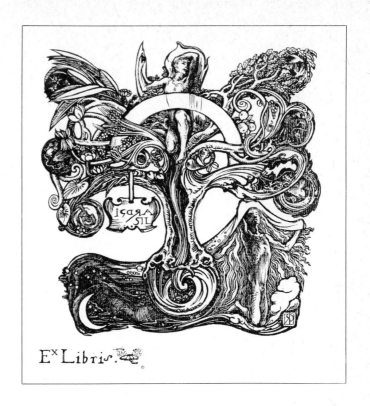

Ex Libris.

CHARLES RICKETTS

Subtle and fantastic decorator

STEPHEN CALLOWAY

FOREWORD BY
KENNETH CLARK

*With 133 illustrations,
6 in color*

THAMES AND HUDSON

for Julia

HALF-TITLE: *Igdrasil*, bookplate for Gleeson White, *c.* 1893.
Wood engraving, 8·0 × 7·5 cm ($3\frac{1}{8}$ × $2\frac{15}{16}$ in.).
FRONTISPIECE: Charles Ricketts by Alphonse Legros,
silverpoint drawing, 1895.
TITLE-PAGE: *Honeysuckle*, original design for a border.

© 1979 Thames and Hudson Ltd, London

Library of Congress Catalog card number 79-3954

Text and monochrome illustrations
printed in Great Britain by BAS Printers Limited,
Over Wallop, Hampshire
Colour illustrations printed in Great Britain by
Balding & Mansell Limited, Wisbech, Cambs.
Bound in Great Britain

CONTENTS

Foreword *by Kenneth Clark*

NYONE WHO KNEW THE WORLD OF ART in the 1920s will remember the enchantment of two brilliant talkers, Roger Fry and Charles Ricketts. They were a complete contrast to one another and, although they were the leading critics of art of their time, I never heard them mention each other's name. Roger Fry lived in two rather grubby rooms in Bloomsbury, furnished with the heavy, ill-made chairs and tables of the Omega workshop. On the walls were a few pictures by his French friends, in which every trace of visual delight had been virtuously suppressed in favour of 'plastic values', rendered in lumpy paint and dull colours. He would have looked with a kind of holy horror at the exquisite lightness of Townshend House, where Ricketts and Shannon lived surrounded by what they would have called pretty things – Greek lekythoi, tanagrettes, Venetian glass, drawings by Hokusai and Persian miniatures. No anxiety about plastic values there: simply delight. One dined with Roger Fry in order to hear him talk about some new discovery, a young French painter, or more probably a poet. The food came from under his bed in the next room. There was plenty of good talk in Townshend House too, but one enjoyed it against a background of visual delights. The dining table appeared to be one vast slab of lapis lazuli (I suppose it was made up of several) at the end of which was a barrage of madonna lilies. I do not remember the food because by the end of the meal I was always tipsy, having had to swallow half a bottle of *orvieto secco*, and several glasses of revolting Italian liqueur which Ricketts drank because of its name, *strega*. No wonder that when Ricketts said 'Come and grub with me' one always said 'Yes', and put off any other engagement.

In contrast to Roger's sonorous monologue, Ricketts' conversation was punctuated by screams of laughter, which shook his small frame, and dervish cries of excitement when some artist was mentioned whom he particularly loved – or loathed. He had very catholic tastes, but knowing (and forgiving) my Bloomsbury background, he enjoyed praising the artists despised in that austere milieu, like Gustave Moreau and Odilon Redon. He was not actually hostile to the Impressionists, but agreed with those French critics who thought that the greatest painter of the late nineteenth century was Puvis de Chavannes, and he would confirm his judgment by pointing to some superb drawings by Puvis in his own collection.

Charles Ricketts in his studio at Townshend House aged about sixty, photograph *c.* 1926.

On those evenings Ricketts did most of the talking. Shannon was quiet and recessive, but his rare interpolations showed good sense and considerable learning. One could see that Ricketts turned to him as to a reasonable wife. They had lived together for almost fifty years. So when I heard that Shannon had fallen off a ladder while hanging a picture and was suffering from a kind of concussion, my heart sank. He had lost the use of his faculties. For months Ricketts hoped that he might regain them, but he never did, and in fact outlived Ricketts by many years.

Ricketts never really recovered from this tragedy. He returned to his first love, book production, and did some stage designs; but the brilliant spark was extinguished.

Historians used to speak of the frivolity of the '90s, and it is true that in a small group the moral earnestness of the mid-nineteenth century was considerably relaxed. But the finer spirits of the time had their own belief, held as seriously as any moral convictions of the mid-Victorians, the belief in beauty. This belief united Ricketts with the man who may be seen as his successful rival, Aubrey Beardsley. No doubt Beardsley was the more original artist; also the more limited. Even if he had lived I doubt if he would have gone much beyond his strictly linear style. Whereas Ricketts painted from a rich palette, and was also an accomplished sculptor in the manner of Rodin. From the point of view of a reputation with posterity, versatility is a dangerous gift, and seems to arouse a sort of jealousy. Ricketts did everything well, bringing to each branch of art or craft a feeling for design, a sympathy with the medium and an inexhaustible gift of invention. And, in addition to his technical endowments, all his work shows the stamp of a superior character. Bernard Shaw described him as 'the noble and generous Ricketts . . . a natural aristocrat as well as a loyal and devoted artist'. And it is perhaps a good thing that he should be remembered in this form. But those of us who knew him will always think first of his laugh, destroying all pomposity and encouraging us to say outrageous things.

'Tout pour L'Art'

HARLES RICKETTS belonged to a generation of English artists and men of letters for whom the cultivation of exquisite taste, refined manners and obscure interests had become almost an end in itself. For many the cult of the exquisite was a fashionable pose, but for Ricketts and his life-long companion, the painter Charles Shannon, it was to provide a complete artistic philosophy. Elaborated over a period of fifty years this approach to art and life is the key to all Ricketts' activities and to the appreciation of an otherwise bewildering range of talents. For he was at times illustrator, book designer, wood engraver, painter, sculptor, designer for the theatre, collector, connoisseur and writer.

But more than this, he was a charismatic figure. A tremendous talker and ready wit, he brought to everything he did, in his work and in his day-to-day existence, an exuberance and prodigious energy. He was perfectly capable of working all day long painting or engraving and then, after dinner, sitting down and writing far into the night, his simple explanation of this being, 'I wake up at night'.

He drew others irresistibly to him. Oscar Wilde was fascinated, became a frequent visitor, and spoke of 'the one house in London where you will never be bored'. Wilde called him 'an orchid', which perfectly expressed his preciousness, but also because, among other interests, Ricketts seemed to know all there was to know about rare and sensitive plants. He was the first to admit that this very diversity would be harmful to his reputation and, writing near the end of his life to Cecil French, he spoke of his 'dual personalities' and suggested in characteristically ironic manner that 'I believe I should have been more fruitful . . . if I could have been cut in half'. This and the inevitable coupling of his name with that of Shannon has tended to obscure his singular gifts, although his contribution in several spheres of art was of the first importance.

In the field of book design he must rank with William Morris as one of the founders of the private press movement and, by avoiding in his work many of the archaic mannerisms of the Kelmscott books, his example has been of more significance for modern typographers. As an illustrator, his influence was, arguably, wider and more beneficial than that of Aubrey Beardsley, whose brief career coincided roughly with the main period of Ricketts' interest in book design. Later, in his work for the theatre, Ricketts anticipated much that was done in Russia by Bakst and others for the *Ballets Russes*, and in England by the more acknowledged pioneer, Edward Gordon Craig.

His unusually deep and catholic knowledge embraced the art of many periods and countries, giving rise to several important books and a series of articles, later collected as *Pages on Art* (1913). Thanks to his formidable connoisseurship he came to be regarded as a leading expert and consequently a force in the English art world of the first decades of this century. He was offered, and refused, the considerable honour of the Directorship of the National Gallery, but sat on a number of committees including that of the National Art Collections Fund. Ricketts was distrustful of politics and of the Art Establishment, and was only belatedly persuaded to accept election to the Royal Academy.

Though he moved in influential circles, he was by temperament unsuited to public life, preferring throughout his career the company of a select group of friends. In particular he seems to have enjoyed the society of writers, with whom he felt an intuitive sympathy. Among these literary friends may be numbered the poets John Gray, 'Michael Field' (Edith Cooper and Katherine Bradley) and W. B. Yeats. Wilde, the apostle of aestheticism, was a most important early friend and patron, about whom Ricketts later wrote a volume of *Recollections* (1932). That other notable Irish playwright of the period, George Bernard Shaw, valued Ricketts highly, as much for his opinions and manners as for his work. He wrote of 'the noble and generous Ricketts who always dealt *en grand seigneur* . . .'

Moving with equal ease among painters and connoisseurs, Ricketts had many friends and some enemies. Of the older generation he had, as a student, met and got to know Lord Leighton, who bought a drawing from him, Edward Burne-Jones, who was encouraging, and James McNeill Whistler, who never encouraged anyone. Of his contemporaries William Rothenstein, Edmund Dulac and Max Beerbohm were allies and Aubrey Beardsley a rather hostile rival. In the art historical world Ricketts came to count as personal friends a number of major critics and several museum curators – Gleeson White, the authority on

The Wood Engraver, a portrait of Ricketts by Charles Shannon, 1894. Lithograph, 17·0 × 17·5 cm ($6\frac{11}{16}$ × $6\frac{7}{8}$ in.). Note the oil lamp and water-filled globe used to focus the light on the wood-block.

illustration; Sydney Cockerell of the Fitzwilliam Museum, Cambridge; Cecil French at South Kensington, who wrote an essay in appreciation of Ricketts' woodcuts; and at the British Museum, Lewis Hind and Laurence Binyon, who combined poetry with the care of prints and drawings. After Ricketts' refusal of the Directorship of the National Gallery his own protégé, C. J. Holmes, once the office boy of the Vale Press, was appointed to fill the politically equivocal post. Ricketts' occasional

encounters with that doyen of connoisseurs, Bernhard Berenson, were not a success. Kenneth Clark, who was present as a young man at one such meeting, recalls (1974) that 'they were so suspicious of each other that they hardly spoke. B. B. was heavily sarcastic, Ricketts screamed the aesthete's scream of embarrassment.'

Ricketts' last years were saddened by a certain sense of failure and neglect, only partly allayed by the devotion and support of a small inner circle of friends. Most important among these were Gordon Bottomley, the dramatist who formed the finest single collection of Ricketts' work, Cecil Lewis, a promising young writer, and Thomas Sturge

Moore, a talented disciple. Sturge Moore was the closest of these friends and the assiduous compiler of Ricketts' letters, journals and writings, and it is to him that we owe most of our knowledge of Charles Ricketts, the man.

Without doubt, however, the crucial friendship of Ricketts' life began at the age of sixteen when he first met Charles Shannon. Sturge Moore wrote in his monograph on his friend (1933) that 'between Ricketts and Shannon existed the most marvellous human relationship that has ever come within my observation, and in their prime each was the others complement, but neither easily indulged the other; their union was more bracing than comfortable.' Their temperaments exactly balanced and each was certainly the greatest influence on the art and life of the other. Thus, in writing of Ricketts, Shannon's name too will inevitably appear throughout these pages. Ricketts records in his diary that J. E. Blanche, the noted French portrait painter, 'when he heard that S[hannon] and I had lived together for twenty years, and that our collection was in common, said, *Mais c'est alors une existence idéale que vous menez, tout pour l'art.*'

Early years

Charles de Sousy Ricketts was born in Geneva on 2 October 1866, the only child of parents with some artistic sensibilities. His father, a naval officer, had a certain skill in depicting landscape in watercolour, but it was the boy's French mother, Hélène de Sousy, who was to be the greater influence in these early years. She was an amateur singer and her talents had been sufficient to attract the attention of Rossini, who declared that 'it was a pity her voice could not be heard upon the stage'. Her voice could, however, be heard constantly in the various Ricketts households, first in a substantial villa in Norwood near the Crystal Palace and later in a respectable stucco terrace in Kensington, called by his father 'the catacombs'. Many of Ricketts' earliest memories were connected with music, and visits to concerts at an early age encouraged a precocious love of opera and the stage which lasted throughout his life.

Foreign travel and long stays on the continent were very much a part of family life; as a child Ricketts lived in France and Italy as much as in England. For a year he attended an ordinary day school in Tours, deep in provincial France, the only formal education he received. An independent child, he spent much time alone and from an early age began the process of educating himself. He was considered too delicate for school and so read, drew and listened to music; he also spent time as opportunity arose 'basking in museums'. At the age of thirteen he was again travelling on the continent with his mother when she died at Genoa en route for Rome, and, returning to England he lived with his father for only three years before becoming an orphan. His grandfather, a rich and benevolent man who had given away a fine collection of Italian pictures, took over responsibility for the youth and allowed him to follow his inclination towards a career in art.

Thus, in 1882, at the age of sixteen, Ricketts found himself apprenticed to the wood-engraver Roberts at the City and Guilds Technical Art School in Kennington Park Road, Lambeth. With a quarterly allowance of £25 and his unusual and precocious background, he quickly found himself an object of curiosity to the other students and emerged as a natural leader both in their intellectual life and their play. In this can be seen the origin of Ricketts' later love, or, as some said, mania for influencing people.

The alliance with Shannon was formed in this year, and soon privileged students were invited to frugal evenings at their digs in Kennington. Here work, talk and organizing a collection of prints began to form the pattern of existence that they would follow with little change as the years proceeded. In the main front room brown paper was pinned to the walls to serve as a background for the ever-changing display of reproductions of favourite paintings and book illustrations, purchased for coppers from the bookstalls as cribs for their own designs. It was said that Ricketts could at this time have compiled a better book on illustration than any other writer, so wide was his knowledge of English and continental work. In this way, with bundles and portfolios of cheap reproductions, began what would become one of the most celebrated private collections assembled this century, a unique collection which came over the years to embrace Old Master drawings, prints and paintings, Greek vases and gems, Egyptian antiquities, notable Persian miniatures, and an important group of Japanese drawings and colour prints.

Having completed their apprenticeships, a decision about the future had to be taken, and in 1887 Ricketts and Shannon crossed to Paris to consult Puvis de Chavannes. The distinguished painter was courteous, receiving them with apologies that he had in hand so little to show them. His advice, however, was that they should not study in France as they had planned, but should return to

London and there commence working as artists. From this time dates the extraordinary agreement made between Ricketts and Shannon to follow what amounted to an artistic programme, whereby Shannon would retire from the world and perfect his technique as a painter, later to re-emerge the complete master. During this period, which they estimated at perhaps five years, Ricketts was to continue work as an illustrator and designer in order to provide the means for this monastic existence dedicated to Art.

The decision to follow this bizarre plan had in some ways quite the contrary effect to that which was intended, for by removing pressure from Shannon, it developed or confirmed in his work a self-indulgent trait. On the other hand, for Ricketts, always the dominant element in the partnership, it provided the stimulus and opportunity to make tremendous advances through his enforced practical dealings with the commercial world of book production, one of the most fertile areas of English design in the late nineteenth century.

Ricketts began to draw for the illustrated journals which had proliferated with the introduction of process-reproduction. It was hack work. These illustrations, the decorative *culs-de-lampe* and eighteenth-century fantasies for the *Magazine of Art* and *Black and White*, are in the Aesthetic Taste or in a hesitant Art Nouveau style. Though conventional they are never entirely without interest. In some of the full-page drawings, such as *Shelley* illustrating a sonnet by Swinburne's guardian, Theodore Watts-Dunton, and in the two designs for *A Nympholept* by Swinburne himself, many of the elements of Ricketts' mature style are already present. In particular in these illustrations may be traced the first unmistakable signs of that wonderfully concentrated detail and surface pattern which characterizes his best work of the next few years, which he called 'filigree . . . an almost Persian finick and finish'.

The culmination of this group of drawings is the well-known *Oedipus and the Sphinx*, commissioned by Lord Leighton. The elderly President of the Royal Academy was in the habit of offering promising young draughtsmen the sum of £5 for a drawing on any subject they chose. His rather touching words to Ricketts were: 'I fear you will not care much for my work, but I am very interested in yours. . . .' The result pleased Lord Leighton greatly and he wrote praising the drawing as 'full of imagination', and for its 'weird charm'. 'It is also', he continued, 'in such passages as . . . the wings of the Sphinx and the hair of Oedipus a marvellous

Charles Shannon, wood engraving by Ricketts after a medallion by Alphonse Legros. Diameter 5·8 cm (2¼ in.). From Ricketts' *A Catalogue of Mr. Shannon's Lithographs*, Vale Press, London 1902.

Charles Ricketts and Charles Shannon, by Sir William Rothenstein, lithograph, 1897. From Rothenstein's series of portraits of his artistic friends; Ricketts is shown holding a wood-block.

piece of penmanship.' It is unashamedly eclectic. In technique the drawing has affinities with Rossetti's early graphic work and with the linear precision of Dürer, both increasingly influential models for Ricketts' drawing style. But although the composition owes much to Ingres' treatment of the same subject, the overall effect is unmistakably the result of study of Gustave Moreau. Ricketts considered this the most perfect of his early drawings and, with an unusual sentimentality, at the sale of Leighton's collection bought it back.

p.12

The Vale and *The Dial*

On their return from Paris, bearing in mind the advice of Puvis de Chavannes, Ricketts and Shannon began to search for rooms and a studio in earnest. Whistler, already an acquaintance, offered them an old house in Chelsea, an 'establishment' for one of his models, the lease of which was now proving an embarrassment to him. Ricketts decided that they should take it, and the two artists quickly set themselves up in the house with which their names have always been most closely associated.

The Vale, as it was called, was one of three Regency houses in a then-rural backwater off the King's Road, described by Edith Cooper in her diary as 'a muddy retreat from the highway, edged by gardens in which snowball-trees grow from the soil like wands that are full of sighing'. Ricketts was undoubtedly the presiding genius, 'an un-aurioled, decadent Christ, who talks fluently with a mere rill of voice', and it was at the Vale that his life took on that quality of aloofness and rarified aestheticism that fortunate visitors would try to describe. 'One has to be on one's rarest behaviour – for nothing ordinary is expected; and a false tone might be an outrage.'

The exterior of the house, which is the subject of Shannon's first lithograph, *The Vale in Snow*, was unremarkable, but inside some vestiges of Whistler's idiosyncratic decorative schemes survived. The walls were distempered yellow and were soon hung with prints by Hokusai. Oscar Wilde admired them on his first visit to the Vale remarking, 'What a charming old house you have, and what delightful Japanese prints – Yes the Japanese understand conciseness and compact design . . . How did you discover the Vale? – I like the name – And you have yellow walls, so have I – Yellow is the colour of joy . . .'

Wilde had come out of curiosity, aroused by a copy of the sumptuous volume which Ricketts and Shannon issued under their own imprint from the Vale in 1889. Called *The Dial*, it was their first independent artistic statement, and for a first essay in

Sappho, by Gustave Moreau, *c.* 1875. Watercolour, 18·4 × 12·4 cm (7¼ × 4⅞ in.). This drawing was once in the possession of the poet John Gray, a close friend during Ricketts' formative years. It was, when Ricketts knew it, and remains one of the few examples of the *Symboliste* painter's work in England.

The Great Worm, coloured lithograph, page size 32·5 × 25·5 cm (12⅘ × 10¹⁄₁₆ in.). After an original design by Ricketts, from *The Dial,* no. 1, The Vale, 1889.

the Art of the Book, unusually successful. Wilde's judgment, which may be apocryphal, is well known: 'It is quite delightful, but don't bring out a second number, all perfect things should be unique.' In fact four more issues appeared irregularly between 1892 and 1897.

The design and layout were their own, as was the risk in publishing in such lavish form a collection of writings and illustrations by then-unknown names. In its typography it owes much to the example of Whistler. Whistler, it has been said, was the first to realize that 'latent in printers' cases lay a multiplicity of new arrangements'. In his own experimental publications, such as the printed version of his lecture, *Mr. Whistler's 'Ten O'clock'*, published privately in 1888, he pioneered an asymmetrical use of type and ornament and the use of unusual materials, such as coarse brown paper wrappers, both of which are novel features of the production of *The Dial*.

Ricketts and Shannon contributed the lion's share of the work reproduced in each number, and, since both began to enter into their full powers as draughtsmen at this time, there is much that is good. The standing of *The Dial* is high amongst the many contemporary illustrated literary periodicals. In its large quarto format, good paper and fine printing it resembles most closely *The Hobby Horse*, produced by members of the Century Guild, but it substitutes for the Arts-and-Crafts earnestness of that journal a more distinctly avant-garde stance. It is full of attitudes and images inspired by continental *Symboliste* ideas, at that time little known outside France and Belgium.

Ricketts, along with others of the Vale circle, was among the very few in England with first-hand knowledge of the work of the various *Symboliste* groups, whose influence pervades the designs and writing in *The Dial*. Other friends, including Arthur Symons, Beardsley's co-editor on *The Savoy*, and W. B. Yeats, writing in *The Dome* and elsewhere, did much to introduce the literature to English readers, whilst Oscar Wilde tried unsuccessfully to gain a wider public for 'Les Jeunes Belges'. Ricketts was well versed in the *Symboliste's* work. His knowledge of continental literature was extraordinary, ranging from Flaubert and Maeterlinck, through the Decadents to Zola, Anatole France and Nietzsche. It was he who introduced Wilde to the writings of Verlaine and Villiers de L'Isle Adam, and Sturge Moore recorded that 'he had canvassed the work of Gauguin, Van Gogh, Cézanne, Rimbaud and Mallarmé before those who wrote them up in this country had heard of them'. Take away the names of Van Gogh and Cézanne, to whom Ricketts became violently opposed, add those of Puvis de Chavannes, Moreau and Rodin, and the modern section of Ricketts' pantheon is complete.

In the first number of *The Dial*, Ricketts is represented by several designs, among them a colour lithograph, *The Great Worm*, which again owes much to Moreau and to Parisian ideas. This reproduction led to attempts at lithography as an autonomous artistic medium, in the manner of Redon and Bresdin, rather than for reproduction. It was an innovation in England at this date. Shannon of course achieved great success with the 'capricious medium', but before this, there is only the isolated example of Whistler. The inclusion of an experimental plate demonstrates the extent to which *The Dial* was for Ricketts very much a place for trying out ideas and for testing work in progress. p.12

For the second number, published in 1892, Ricketts re-designed and re-engraved the cover. Influenced by Rossetti and, in its details, by Dürer, the revised version shows a greater awareness of proportion and clarity. It is in this sense more typographical and, by introducing an element of restraint, it represents the next stage in Ricketts' stylistic development. His most important contribution to the second number, however, was a piece of writing, a defence of the principles of the first number of *The Dial* which forms a manifesto for the Aesthetic ideal. As such it deserves to be far better known and justifies quotation at length. It appeared with a large decorative head-piece under the title 'The Unwritten Book'. 10

'The accusation was brought against our first Dial of mere art eclecticism; one thing, keenly attractive to us, might explain this reprehensible selectiveness, a little thing we think common to all good art. Inseparable from the garment of individuality, the word *Document* perfectly explains this.

Record of some remembered delight, record perhaps of a mere moment in transfigured life, producing and controlling it, the word *Document* represents some exquisite detail in a masterpiece, convincing to the spectator as a thing known yet not of necessity the symbol of borrowed story — possibly, there, the mere symbol of time. A thing easily imagined away from a picture, but authoritative there, as a gesture, or poetical recollection; the lattice-light cast upon the wall in Rossetti's Proserpina might be chosen to prove that *Document* is not necessarily the mere machinery giving vraisemblance to positive subject, for . . . [this] picture is almost without it. . . .

The fateful pomegranate might however be put into the hand of many an Italian portrait, the title Donna Innominata painted on the frame would not destroy this picture's memorableness — to-morrow the name Proserpine might be given to Da Vinci's Mona Lisa, and so, seemingly, unseal its secret. In Whistler's White Harmony the sub-ject is intentionally fugitive. . . .

These works have been chosen for their lack of story, in its common acceptance; and so we come easily to the colour exclamation on some Chinese enamel, dabbed there in vibrant crimson on a liquid purple, where no subject can exist at all; yet this thing, by its cunning spontaneity, will give the emotion that sudden movement adds to nature — the ripple of grass in a summer land-scape for instance — and so become *Document* — that monument of moods. A viol left on a lower-ing bow by some singer who has ceased, one mari-gold drowned in a space of water, would convey, within a picture and without, this sense of exis-tence and prëexistence, this sense of time.

In the work of the English Pre-Raphaelites, *Document* has been chiselled in new-cleft gems; in Impressionism, it has been wrapped in strokes that waved into air, or that palpitated into light; far be it then from us to claim it treasure trove. . . . We make no claim to originality, . . . for all art is but the combination of known quantities, the interplay of a few senses only; . . . We would therefore avoid all taint of announced reform for those pathetically persistent in demanding it; . . . Art has been, Art is. . . .

One word more of apology.

All past effort has seemed more conscious of aim, more direct, than it was really; we imagine an effort towards renaissance, springing from a white hand beckoning above the ashes of some forgotten city, and seen at some time by one in whom the possible germ of a new art was placed. . . . We forget those previous years, wasted in barren yearning, satisfied at last by something con-temporary. . . . To-day the announcement that you believe in Nature, or in Ideas, affords claim to originality, and we would avoid this announce-ment . . . let admiration be one of the reasons for the Dial to exist; admiration . . . is 'the essence of all art' — it is that which makes us wish in childhood, when power is not yet, and before ex-perience has shut the gates, for larger flowers. . . . Let the great artists yet alive be witness that copy-book culture is the only reason for this colourless currency in art and thought; the rainbow of Art is still there for Hope to look through, . . . Art has been, Art is, so the present touches wings with the past.

Slowly the old fantastic details of primitive art return, with these, the old ornamentalness; lyrical movement recoils, becomes arrested, a tense im-mobility ensues, more ultimate than the great calm of the Antique, for upon the Parthenon, the great divine limbs leap and rebound, the draperies cling close to flesh, deep with the possibility of sweat.'

Book designer and illustrator

The advent of Oscar Wilde at the Vale brought not only an improvement in the standards of conversation and dress there, but far more importantly the opportunity for Ricketts to work as a practical book designer and illustrator on books suited to his talents. Wilde was just entering upon the period when most of his major works were being published and Ricketts, with occasional help from Shannon, was responsible for the appearance of them all, with the exception of *Salomé* (designed and illustrated by Beardsley).

It had all begun with a light-hearted commission for Ricketts to paint an imaginary 'portrait of Mr. W. H.' to serve as frontispiece to Wilde's story of that name. Ricketts' picture of 'Will Hewes' was painted in a fortnight 'on a decaying piece of oak' and 'framed . . . in a fragment of worm-eaten moulding, which . . . Shannon pieced together'. It delighted the author. He wrote, 'It is not a forgery at all — it is an authentic Clouet of the highest artistic value. It is absurd of you and Shannon to try and take me in — as if I did not know the master's touch or was no judge of frames!' The edition did not appear and sadly the original panel has never been seen since it was knocked down for a guinea at the terrible dispersal of Wilde's goods during his trial in April 1895.

Other projects had more tangible outcomes. In 1891 four of Wilde's books were published in bindings designed by Ricketts, already recognizable for their eccentricity. *The Picture of Dorian Gray* had a white parchment spine with title and author's name stamped at the foot and *Intentions*, bound in dull green cloth bore the titles of the four essays in hand-drawn lettering based on Rossetti's version of William Blake's script. Ricketts later came to regret these eccentricities in his early commercial work and the influence which they had.

23

The most important of this early group of books for Wilde is *The House of Pomegranates*. Ricketts provided a beautiful title-page; again Rossettian, it shows a queen embroidering. As a conceit the designs which she works are the small page ornaments in the book. The title-page states: 'The design and decoration of this book by C. Ricketts and C. H. Shannon', but in fact Shannon's contribution was limited to the four full-page plates, which, printed in Paris by a new and imperfect process, rapidly faded to near invisibility. What remains is a splendidly ornamented book with twelve illustrations and numerous decorations by Ricketts.

The cover came in for much abuse, which provoked Wilde's celebrated reply to the critic of *The Speaker*:

'It is to Mr. Ricketts that the entire decorative design of the book is due, from the selection of the type and the placing of the ornamentation, to the completely beautiful cover that encloses the whole. The writer [in *The Speaker*] . . . does not 'like the cover'. This is no doubt to be regretted, though it is not a matter of much importance, as there are only two people in the world whom it is absolutely necessary that the cover should please. One is Mr. Ricketts, who designed it, the other is myself, whose book it binds. We both admire it immensely!'

In addition to these books Ricketts designed several others for the firm of Osgood McIlvaine and Co., to whom Wilde had introduced him, including two by Hardy: *A Group of Noble Dames* (1891) and the famous *Tess of the D'Urbervilles* (1891). In 1892 the firm ceased and Ricketts as a designer followed Wilde to new publishers: the partnership of Elkin Mathews and John Lane, at the sign of the Bodley Head, where much that was most interesting in literature of the 1890s would find its way into print, often in elegant editions.

With Mathews and Lane, Ricketts designed and illustrated a number of interesting books. For a new edition of Wilde's *Poems* (1892) he produced the most satisfying of his ornate bindings. The design, known as *The Seven Trees*, was blocked in gold on fine lilac cloth, and in it Ricketts shows himself to be the complete master of the die-stamped binding. Rossetti too had distinguished himself in this medium. Although Ricketts knew Rossetti's books, their influence was to be more important for him later. Gleeson White, himself a good designer of bindings, in an article on Ricketts in *The Pageant* (1896) wrote,

Cover for *Poems*, by Oscar Wilde; Elkin Mathews and John Lane, London 1892. Pale lilac cloth, blocked in gold with the design, *The Seven Trees*, 21·7 × 14·2 cm (8½ × 5⅞ in.).

'Cloth binding, but latterly a thing of horror has suddenly become illuminated with intelligence; and for this no second name need be coupled with that of Mr. Ricketts. In his decorations for many modern books . . . he has set up new standards that have largely been appreciated, and unluckily as largely imitated. Take for instance a beautiful cover to one of these books, with its rigidly symmetrical trees, and you will see that a distinctly eastern flavour pervades it, yet the spirit of the Renaissance infuses all to a sober simplicity.'

More bindings followed in this vein, notably that for J. A. Symonds' *In the Key of Blue* (1893) and for Lord de Tabley's *Poems Dramatic and Lyrical* (1893), covers which 'contain an entire rule of [Ricketts'] own as to how metal stamps should be understood in the decoration of a book'. The *Poems* of de Tabley were published in an edition limited to six hundred copies. It is the last of Ricketts' works where the pictures are directly inspired by Pre-Raphaelite illustration, particularly Rossetti's, and by Dürer. In the frontispiece, *The Defeat of Glory,* and in *The Two Old Kings,* there is the unmistakable influence of Rossetti's elaborate pen drawings of Romantic subjects in enclosed medieval settings of the 1850s, whilst the most powerful image of the five, *Nimrod,*

15

shows in its 'finick and finish' Ricketts' admiration for Rossetti's famous illustration of St Cecilia for *The Palace of Art* in the Moxon edition of *Poems by Alfred Tennyson* (1857). The *Knight in the Wood* recalls Dürer, but a Dürer interpreted by Burne-Jones. In it too may be traced the 'old fantastic details of primitive Art' of which Ricketts had written in *The Dial*. Here, and in other of his illustrations, there are echoes of paintings Ricketts knew in the National Gallery, for the knight surrounded by such intricate leaves and tiny animals is surely a distant recollection of Pisanello's *Vision of St Eustace*.

Two final examples of Ricketts' commercial work will serve to show less his protean stylistic development than his unparalleled ability to create variety of effect in book design. He was unique among designers in this varying of the treatment to suit the subject and 'feel' of the writing.

Silverpoints, a small volume of poems by John Gray, an intimate of the Vale circle and a contributor to *The Dial*, appeared in 1893, the cost of its publication being underwritten by Oscar Wilde. It was the most inventive of Ricketts' books to date and, in its distinguished effect produced with such economy of means, his most sophisticated. The tall, narrow format was based on the Persian 'saddle-book', reflecting both the 'exquisite' quality of the poetry and the more practical consideration that a favourite book of poems should be easy to carry in the pocket. The text was set throughout in italic type with simple initials for which, in Ricketts' words, 'the model . . . was one of those rare Aldus italic volumes with its margins uncut'. The total effect is one of elegant proportion and lightness, perfectly recalling the Venetian original. The cover, of green cloth with an all-over pattern in gilt of wavy lines subtly strewn with leaves and interrupted only by a tiny panel for the title, was influential and much imitated – drifting back to him, Ricketts wrote, 'from places where my name is quite unknown; on bindings, end-papers, wall papers and dress cretonnes'.

The last book to be considered in this group is widely held to be Ricketts' finest. This is *The Sphinx* (1894) by Oscar Wilde. Ricketts had full control of the design and format, illustration and arrangement of the type; the use of rich materials, good paper and fine vellum mirrors precisely the exotic and perverse qualities of Wilde's poem. Ricketts explained the curious 'build' thus:

'This is the first book of the modern revival of printing printed in red, black and green; the small bulk of the text and unusual length of the lines necessitated quite a peculiar arrangement; here I made an effort away from the Renaissance towards a book marked by surviving classical traits, printing it in Capitals.'

These long lines of small capital letters, the drawn initial letters, and exactly judged interplay between illustration and text do in fact combine to give something of the feel of an early manuscript. There is no conventional title-page, but rather a double-opening which gives the details of publication and begins the text; and here the combination of colours, dull brownish red and a pale sage green with the black, enhances the decorative quality of well-arranged type.

Ricketts considered the illustrations his finest and most lyrical drawings but Wilde, surprisingly, did not agree: 'No my dear Ricketts, [they] are not of your best. You have seen them through your intellect, not your temperament.' For Ricketts the attempt had been to combine the best qualities of line work of many epochs to 'evolve what one might imagine as possible in one charmed moment or place'. The drawings achieve this timeless rarified atmosphere; they have a hieratic quality and the sense is conveyed of ritual action arrested at the very moment when the composition of the elements is perfect.

Robert Ross, Wilde's literary executor, gave to the British Museum Ricketts' original page layouts for the book and the Fitzwilliam Museum has two of the finished drawings. In sepia ink on pink prepared paper they have an even greater nervous quality of line than the process blocks. Drawings exist, too, for the binding, which is Japanese in inspiration. It is of fine white vellum and the designs on front and back cover and spine are drawn with the same tense and intricate line; blocked in gold they complete the sense of decadent luxury which the book exudes.

Now so highly regarded, *The Sphinx* did not sell well on publication. Ready for publication in 1893, it was postponed for a year in order not to clash with *Salomé*. The *succès de scandale* of Beardsley's illustrations overshadowed the publication of *The Sphinx* and like *A House of Pomegranates,* which was remaindered, a large proportion of the edition of two hundred copies remained unsold. These were destroyed in a fire at the Ballantyne Press in 1899 (along with other books and many of Ricketts' engraved wood-blocks), with the result that *The Sphinx* is not only the most splendid of Ricketts' early books, but also the rarest.

Private press work

Though Ricketts was moving towards complete control of the various elements in the make-up of a book, he was unaware at this time of William Morris' attempts in 1888 at the Chiswick Press to use an ordinary commercial printing firm, albeit one with a good typographical tradition, to produce acceptably artistic books. Only partly successful, Morris' *The House of the Wolfings* and *The Roots of the Mountains* are really the first books of the modern movement. 'These might have initiated me at the time to a better and more severe style,' Ricketts later wrote.

By 1891 Morris had taken the desire for control of the processes of book production to its logical conclusion by setting up his own press and printing, by hand, from his own type and wood-blocks. Although Ricketts was the first to follow Morris' lead and eventually established a private press of his own in 1896, he was not at this stage ready to take an entirely independent course. In fact he wrote that he did not immediately appreciate the Kelmscott books: 'I am now puzzled that my first impression of *The Glittering Plain*, the first Kelmscott book, was one of disappointment.'

At the same time as working for the commercial publishing world Ricketts was also engaged on a more long-term and private plan. He had projected, with the collaboration of Shannon, a large book illustrated throughout with pictures and initial letters engraved by themselves and printed from the wood, in conscious emulation of the old Venetian books which they admired. The particular model for their project was the *Hypnerotomachia Poliphili* (The Strife of Love, revealed in a Dream by Poliphilus), printed in Venice by Aldus in 1499. Recognized as one of the unsurpassed masterpieces of printing, the *Hypnerotomachia* had been mentioned by several writers, and the pages of the book which bore illustrations had been reproduced in facsimile, making the basic format and the placing of the pictures in relation to type familiar. Ricketts was fortunate enough to own an original edition.

The subject which Ricketts chose to treat in this way was the story of *Daphnis and Chloe* by the late Classical writer Longus, in a Jacobean version which Shannon and he had discovered, 'done into English by George Thornley, Gent.' There are thirty-seven illustrations and over one hundred engraved initials in the book, and this ambitious scale meant a long period of painstaking work: 'the engraving alone of the pictures and initials occupied us for eleven months'. For the illustrations Shannon made fifteen designs, the rest being by Ricketts, who for consistency of effect drew them all on to the wood-blocks. Both then engraved, Ricketts most of the initials, and Shannon therefore the major part of the pictures. Some blocks, including that for Ricketts' illustration *The Love of Venus for Anchises*, survive and are preserved in the British Museum Print Room. 41, 42

William Rothenstein who knew the two artists at this time has recorded how, 'bending over their blocks . . . [they] looked like figures from a missal'. Ricketts in this characteristic position is the subject, too, of one of Shannon's splendid portrait lithographs, *The Wood Engraver,* of 1894. Sturge Moore p.9 has described Ricketts' method of work when designing a wood-block. This involved endlessly re-drawing the design on both sides of a sheet of thin paper until the basic arrangement was satisfactory, when it would be pasted down to a firm card backing and squared for transfer to the block. Some drawings at this stage survive. Once the design was set out on the block, but before cutting commenced, Ricketts would become absorbed in moving tiny pieces of paper over the surface of the wood with a pin, trying out minute alterations; according to Sturge Moore, 'Actual sensuous proportions were in question, however slight.'

Work was completed on the *Daphnis and Chloe* blocks in 1893. Painstakingly supervised by Ricketts, the type was set up at the Ballantyne Press section by section and the book slowly printed off. It was issued in a small edition by Mathews and Lane and was well received. Undoubtedly it was, with the exception of Morris' Kelmscott books, the most serious and most successful attempt at that date to revive the fine printing of the early illustrated books.

Five years later Ricketts looked critically at this early performance, writing

'I still view this work with great affection, though . . . overcrowded by initials and lines in capitals, that overset at times the proper balance between the illustrations and the text in a manner not foreseen by us. I hope someday to reprint this wonderful and unknown English text, with those amendments in type and design that I have now won by experience in the handling of books.'

The edition sold out quickly enough to justify the production of another volume, and *Hero and Leander* by Christopher Marlowe and George Chapman was selected. The smaller scale of the text allowed Ricketts to devote more attention to details, so from

Daphnis to *Hero* there are some significant advances. It becomes clear that from this time Ricketts was in effect operating his own private press. The paper on which the book was printed was specially made and bears a watermark of the letters VP for Vale Press interlaced with a leaf of wild thyme. In the final colophon these appear again with the initials S and R for Shannon and Ricketts.

The seven illustrations are contemporary with the designs for *The Sphinx* and have similar intensity and weird charm; as in *The Sphinx,* illustration and type balance in weight exactly. There is a further advance in the quality of the typography and Ricketts' distinctive paragraph mark of a leaf makes its first appearance. The type is still, of course, a commercial old-fashioned Caslon pica and it is effectively only this which distinguishes the book from the true productions of the Vale Press. Writing in 1899, Ricketts noted with satisfaction, '[it] is well printed and in margin and proportion of page quite what I would do now'. As with many of Ricketts' editions there was a small number of copies (in this case six) in a special binding. Vellum was used, tooled in gold and 'in blind' with an abstract arabesque design, which, like the later special bindings, seems to owe more to Rossetti's example than the commercial books had done.

From this point in Ricketts' career as a 'builder of books' it has been customary to judge all his activities exclusively in terms of the private press movement in which he played such a conspicuous part. This is a mistake, since the work he did for his own press was an extension of his practice when designing for others. His contacts with the commercial world were not entirely severed and his keen interest in the work of fellow artists continued. There is a curious similarity between one of the *Hero* designs, *Coyness and Love,* by Ricketts, and Beardsley's drawing *The Mysterious Rose Garden* in *The Yellow Book* (vol. 4, 1895). This one brief comparison must stand for many that could be made between Ricketts and several of the illustrators and designers of the 1890s.

The Vale Press

With the completion of *Hero and Leander* in 1894 Ricketts had reached the point where the design of a new and personal typeface became a prerequisite for further progress. 'I felt that whatever the effort made in design and ornament, the poverty of the founts I had used was a thing not to be discounted.' Even with a legacy of £500, however, Ricketts' means were insufficient to enable him to set up independently with his own types; it was the timely intervention of Rothenstein which helped launch the Vale Press. Rothenstein introduced Ricketts to Llewellyn Hacon, a rich lawyer. More interested in art than the law, Hacon was willing to advance the necessary capital of £1000 in exchange for a 'vague understanding' about a half share in the profits, if any, from the enterprise.

The first fount of type, the Vale, was designed in the long dark room used by Ricketts as a studio in the house in Beaufort Street, to which he and Shannon had moved in 1894. Drawn out with a brush and cut by Mr W. Prince, a professional die-cutter, the new type was ready by 1896. The Ballantyne Press was still to be employed to carry out the actual printing, but now a hand press and a press-man were to be reserved there for the use of Ricketts alone. With the acquisition of shop premises in Warwick Street off Regent Street, duly adorned with the signboard, 'At the sign of the Dial' painted by Shannon (now in Aberdeen Art Gallery), the Vale Press could truly be said to exist.

So much paper has been covered in discussion of the aims and achievements of the private press movement that it seems best here to concentrate on the details of Ricketts' practice, outlining its similarities to and differences from that of Morris, where these are significant.

The guiding principle of the Press was Ricketts' dictum that 'A certain amount of fine literature, owing to its quality of permanence, suggests for that reason the desirability of a beautiful and permanent form for it.' There was also the consideration that the classics had a wider appeal and if care was taken to choose texts for which there was a need, then the risk involved in publication could be minimized. For this reason the original plan did not include the publication of new writings. Ricketts did in fact produce a number of books by his friends John Gray, 'Michael Field' and Sturge Moore, but prudently turned down Wilde's proposal that he should print *The Portrait of Mr W. H.*, a decision for which he later felt pangs of guilt.

The first book, *The Early Poems of John Milton,* was issued in 1896, and this was followed by a series of editions of the earlier poets, including Suckling, Campion and Sydney, which were edited by Gray. All these volumes follow a basic pattern not unlike the Kelmscott books. They have no title-page, beginning with the text on the first page, occasionally opposite an illustration. This first opening (double-page spread) and some others have elaborate borders inspired by plant forms, in their

51

52/56

50

p.19

conception and execution lighter and more natural,
istic than those of Morris. The principal difference
from Morris is that the ornamentation and design of
the book is varied to suit the text. Thus some, such
as *The Rowley Poems of Thomas Chatterton* (1898),
have a dainty and almost whimsical feeling, whilst
others, including the series of 'Michael Field's'
writings, have the robust sombre quality of the
Renaissance borders in sixteenth-century Italian
and German books.

The greatest triumphs of the Press are those in
which Ricketts' illustrations appear throughout the
text. Many of the best drawings, such as those for the
two versions of *Cupid and Psyche* (English and
Latin) and the unused designs for the *Kingis Quair,*
are early in conception and were only given their
settings some time later. For Ricketts became
increasingly interested in typography. Two further
founts of type were designed, the Avon, a smaller
version of the Vale, and the King's Fount, a curious,
experimental alphabet in which uncial forms
replace the familiar Roman shapes of the letters.
Being novel in design the King's Fount was of
course roundly abused by critics along with other of
Ricketts' mannerisms in the arrangement of type.

In 1898 Ricketts collaborated with Lucien
Pissarro to write an essay entitled *De la typographie et
de l'harmonie de la page imprimée; William Morris et son
influence sur les arts et métiers,* many of the ideas of
which he elaborated in the more polemical *A
Defence of the Revival of Printing* (1899). The
collaboration with Pissarro, the son of the
Impressionist painter, was for a time fruitful.
Ricketts allowed Pissarro to use the Vale type for his
early experiments, before the latter produced the
Brook type for his own Eragny Press. Pissarro's
more colourful style seems to have influenced
Ricketts to substitute for the sober blue-grey boards
and simple title-labels of the early Vale books the
distinctive patterned papers which he became so
good at designing.

In 1899 the Vale Press suffered a terrible set-back
from which it was never to recover. This was the fire
at the Ballantyne Press. It destroyed many books,

Coyness and love strive which hath greater grace, wood
engraving, 8·3 × 8·0 cm (3¼ × 3⅓ in.). From Marlowe's
Hero and Leander, Elkin Mathews and John Lane, London
1894.

The Mysterious Rose Garden, by Aubrey Beardsley, *c.* 1894.
Line block, 16·2 × 8·8 cm (6⅜ × 3 7/16 in.). From *The
Yellow book,* vol. 4, London January 1895. The similarities
between this and the previous illustration are striking. The
two are exactly contemporary.

The Man in the Inverness Cape, a portrait of Charles Ricketts, by Charles Shannon, 1897. Oil on canvas, 95·3 × 99 cm (37½ × 39 in.).

but far worse, most of Ricketts' engraved blocks of initial letters and the beautiful borders, each of which had taken three or four weeks to design and cut. Ricketts calculated that a whole year's work would not replace what was gone; 'the loss of my little stock seemed almost irreparable'. With the destruction of most of the ornaments, the last Vale Press books took on a new and beautiful austerity. Decoration is reduced to a minimum; the placing of type becomes everything. Where there are illus-trations, as in the splendid set of ten blocks for *The Parables,* which relate closely to Ricketts' work as a painter, they appear unadorned in simple relation to the text. The last major undertaking of the Press was an edition of Shakespeare in thirty-seven volumes, for which Ricketts conceived a spare and severely elegant format which greatly influenced the later development of the private press movement.

Ricketts announced that, with the completion of the Shakespeare, the Vale Press would close. He printed as a farewell a *Bibliography* which has as its frontispiece a cut of the signboard showing the Dial and Shannon's design of Pegasus grazing in an enclosed paddock, tended by a woman with a bough. Ricketts' achievement had been enormous. Over eighty books had been issued, all directly supervised at the Press by him. A vast number of initials, borders and illustrations had been designed, and in the main cut by him alone, and a whole new range of styles for book production had been established. It was to him as much as to Morris that

future designers would look. Indeed his work as a typographer alone would be enough to give him an important place among English artists and de-signers.

On closing the Vale Press, Ricketts consigned the type matrices to the Thames, 'As it is undesirable that these founts should drift into hands other than their designer's and become stale by unthinking use.' In this began the tradition for private presses to cease completely. The act was symbolic and not without poignancy, for the Press had been a happy enterprise. Ricketts wrote of his last visit to the Ballantyne office to supervise the printing of the *Bibliography* on vellum sheets, describing how the press-men shook his hand with tears in their eyes; 'I was quite touched, and realised that I was bidding good-bye to a portion of my life.'

Painter in oils

With the winding up of the Vale Press and a temporary waning of his interest in the illustration and design of books, Ricketts turned to the problems of oil painting. Shannon by this time was making considerable progress as a painter and enjoying some small measure of success and critical approval. Thus the time had come by the terms of their artistic programme for Ricketts too to devote his energies to the Fine Arts. Whistler had been, according to Sir Edmund Davis, 'vastly struck' with one of Shannon's paintings, *Les Marmitons,* 'returning to it again and again, with the excla-mation "How is it done?" '.

This very question lies at the heart of Ricketts' approach to painting. For he was of the opinion that great art in all periods was the result of the intelligent study of the art of the past. Ricketts advocated a minute and painstaking investigation of the techniques employed by the masters; throughout his life much of his talk and writing was concerned with this technical appreciation of works of art. Ricketts and Shannon were widely held to be the most knowledgeable and eclectic of modern painters, although the value of this knowledge was sometimes questioned. Though their work was once accused of being mere art history, dry scholarship was always tempered with an emotional response, with a real reverence for the Old Masters. For Ricketts the element of connoisseurship gradually outpaced the creative impulse towards painting. The most tangible results of his intense study of their most revered painters – Velasquez and the Venetians – were the substantial survey of the

Prado (1904) and the still-useful monograph on *Titian* (1910).

Painting never seems to have been an entirely satisfactory medium for Ricketts. The entries in his journals reveal that the main problems were technical:

'I fear I am probably now at that stage of develop-ment as a painter when progress is slow, if indeed there is progress at all. When one is a beginner, it is delightful to develop one's power of rapid sketching. Then follows the heart rending period when decision has to be shown in the painting of an eye-socket, the cartilage of a nose, in those hundred things in which colours become muddy and form eludes one's brush.'

Again in a revealing letter to Cecil French written late in life, Ricketts explained: 'My painting refuses to face detail and certain kinds of invention, which Moreau or Burne-Jones have at their finger tips.' His acute critical sense lays bare the exact weakness in his painting. In terms of design and colour arrangement many of his canvasses could be very distinguished, but few in fact achieve real success. He comes nearest to realizing the promise of his graphic work where he most nearly approaches this 'invention' of Moreau and Burne-Jones, and achieves that inner consistency of subject and treatment which he admired in Rossetti and in the monumental *Symboliste* works of Puvis de Chav-annes. Where he relies on a painterly atmospheric effect based on Titian, the Venetians and G. F. Watts, his productions are least interesting.

For Ricketts the details and subject of an oil painting were not the only important con-siderations; the physical act of painting, the actual manipulation of paint as colour and texture, mattered too. But the subject was a starting point from which the artist began. Ricketts was interested only in figure subjects, both in his work and in the work of others, for all other types of painting such as landscape and still-life were considered inferior and less serious. He had a predeliction for elaborately worked out iconographical arrangements but again insisted that what was important in them was the artist's mental process: 'I believe all allegories are only intelligible at the moment they are thought of and, in many works of Art, the original intention becomes obscured by its development: as a piece of music which often means several things.'

Ricketts liked to keep his paintings in the studio for a very long time, not working consistently but returning to them periodically, making small alterations in particular to the accents and high-lights. So cerebral was the process that often these changes were tried on the glass of the frame before being actually hazarded on the canvas. He returned again and again to treat a few subjects which absorbed him: the legend of *Don Juan*, a few episodes in the life of Christ and the *Parables* and the story of *Montezuma,* on whose life he encouraged Cecil Lewis to write a play, never produced, for which he designed costumes and settings. II, III

What becomes clear is that for Ricketts painting was a process involving philosophical speculation, a sort of meditation or spiritual exercise. In discussion with Yeats, Ricketts had formulated a theory that, although 'great natural talents and ability . . . are fairly common, what constitutes the superiority of the really talented man is his own sense of the importance of his gifts.' Ricketts had fatal doubts about his ability and value as a painter and this lack of conviction blights much of his work. In some instances, as for example in the splendid *Death of Montezuma* and in a few of the *Don Juan* and I biblical scenes, a passionate concern for the subject at last overcomes the hesitancy and the work is brought to a satisfactory conclusion.

New directions

In 1902 Ricketts and Shannon moved to Lans-downe House near Holland Park, to studios which had been built with them in mind by Sir Edmund Davis, the South African millionaire, a new friend and patron. Here and at Davis' house, across the road, Ricketts began to widen his acquaintanceship with the London art world. New friends and new interests were quickly acquired and as quickly assimilated. No doubt in part out of dissatisfaction with painting he moved rapidly from one activity to another, and it is from this time that his great natural talents became to some extent dissipated in a harmful diversity.

At different times sculpture, lithography, design-ing jewellery and working as a designer for the stage were all fitted into the day's schedule; so too were committee meetings and exhibition work for the International Society and the Society of Twelve, writing, which became an important source of income, and the continual pursuit of objects for the ever-growing collection. In each of the different spheres of activity Ricketts achieved something and each warrants mention, if only to demonstrate his grasp of the various media. Sturge Moore writing of this understanding called him 'matchless in his

August, by Charles Shannon. Chiaroscuro woodcut, diameter 13·5 cm (5⅜ in.). Published in *The Artist Engraver,* London 1904. Working within a circular format seems to have fascinated Ricketts and Shannon. This design is one of a series intended for the decoration of ceramic plates.

intuitive recognition of the capabilities of different materials and in his power of designing in perfect harmony with the demands they make.' Design is the key word.

If Ricketts took up sculpture and attempted lithography to serve as a relief from the frustrations of painting, in modelling he found a medium which was to help him explore the problems of represent-ing the Form which eluded his paint-brush. He claimed to be the man who best knew and understood Rodin's work; meeting the master at Davis' house revived his desire to attempt three-dimensional pieces of his own. As early as 1900 he had written, 'the sight of [Rodin's] things stirred up curious old wishes of mine to do sculpture', and when he came to produce the delightful series of small bronzes of Romantic subjects the influence of the great sculptor was clear. These bronzes remain, however, closely related to Ricketts' other work. He would treat most readily favourite poetic themes such as *Paulo and Francesca,* in which the figures combine to form a circle, a conceit which recalls Dante's divisions of Purgatory. Sometimes there are references to earlier designs such as in the beautiful single standing figure, *Silence,* which is based on one of the page ornaments in *A House of Pomegranates* drawn fifteen years previously.

75
20

The element of design is always predominant and the rippling forms are made to fit a pre-conceived pattern. Henry Poole, the sculptor, noticed this sense of organization of shapes when he

remarked, 'whatever may be said about that fellow's anatomy, no matter from where you look at his statuettes you see a telling silhouette, and it is only great masterpieces that rival him in that.'

Experiments with lithography, the medium in which Shannon so excelled, were very un-satisfactory and although a few good images resulted – rather like the work of Redon – Ricketts did not persevere. 'The tiresome thing about a new medium is that old failings return. ... Lithographs !!! – Shan't go on.' The example which pleased him most was used as a poster advertising Thomas Hardy's monumental drama, *The Dynasts.*

7

7

Jewellery designing was taken up not as a serious artistic pursuit, but more as a result of Ricketts' natural generosity and love of distributing gifts. All the pieces made to his designs were conceived for their recipients – Shannon, Edith Cooper, Mrs Hacon and Mrs Binyon and May Morris, for whom elements in the designs would have special significance. A book of designs for jewellery by Ricketts in the British Museum has a number of drawings which show great refinement and in-vention.

V
7

Ricketts' method of designing these pieces was similar to the way in which he composed a wood-block or finished an oil painting. The stones to be set were laid out on paper and moved around until a pleasant and telling arrangement was found, and the form of the setting was then indicated in pencil and watercolour – the 'subject' sometimes emerging accidently by chance suggestions of shapes. Several of these pieces survive, including the *Pegasus* pendant which frames Ricketts' only painted portrait, a miniature made for Edith Cooper. Although the execution was often too coarse to satisfy Ricketts' exacting standards, the jewels are wholly successful, evoking the colourful and robust charm of Renaissance gems.

7

2,

The other major activity of this period, designing for the stage, was in a similar way taken up lightheartedly at first and remained to some extent, in Sturge Moore's words, 'a holiday task'. Yet for Ricketts stage-design quickly assumed a consider-able importance. His love of the theatre coupled with his facility in drawing made him ideally suited to the visualizing of costumes and settings; but, more than this, he rapidly became one of the most able practical workers on the stage. Coming late to theatrical design at the age of forty he assumed a position in the forefront of alert taste and found himself in demand with many of the most important theatrical figures of the day.

Within the scope of these pages only the briefest

outline of Ricketts' career in the theatre can be given, for between 1906 and his death in 1931 he was involved, in varying degrees, with over fifty productions. For some of these he contributed only a single costume, while for others he had complete control of every aspect. Often he became involved in the labour not only of producing hundreds of working drawings but also of stencilling costumes, making properties and even painting scenery and physically dressing and lighting the stage. Often the designs became highly finished watercolours.

The first projects with which he was concerned were small semi-professional productions of Sturge Moore's *Astarte* and of *The Dark Lady of the Sonnets,* which began his fruitful association with George Bernard Shaw. This was to ripen into an invigorating friendship and lead to the famous production of *St Joan.* Also from this date there are designs for a projected staging of *Salomé,* which had once been discussed with Wilde back in the days of the Vale.

Ricketts as a designer came before a wider public first in 1909 with Herbert Trench's production of *King Lear* at the Haymarket Theatre, and from this date he was fairly extensively employed in large productions. His talents, of course, lay in the design of settings and costumes of an exotic, mythological or timeless nature, and so his most effective work was for plays such as *The Winter's Tale,* produced by Granville Barker in 1912, and *Salomé,* for which he finally mounted a production in Tokyo in 1919. Yet larger-scale productions came near the end of his career and *St Joan* in 1924 was perhaps the finest of these. For this he made minute preparations, even going so far as to illuminate pages of St Joan's missal although it would never be opened on stage, just as he once illuminated a page of *Hero and Leander* in emulation of some early pious craftsman.

Theatre design is a transient art form, and Ricketts' contribution is difficult to evaluate. We must take on trust the contemporary opinion that the productions were often splendid, but what remains is a glorious series of drawings for costumes and settings, none finer than those intended for the production, never mounted, of Cecil Lewis' *Montezuma,* dating from the early 1920s.

Ricketts' reputation as a stage designer has not endured and Edward Gordon Craig, who wrote more but did so much less, is today more highly regarded. Ricketts had no high opinion of Craig, finding him 'intelligent but diffuse'. Of his relationship to the other great designer in similar vein, Leon Bakst, whose work he greatly admired, Ricketts has left an honest evaluation; replying to

Ricketts and Shannon as Indian gods, by Edmund Dulac, *c.*1914. Gouache, diameter 29·9 cm (11¼ in.). One of Dulac's meticulous caricatures of his friends in fanciful roles. The scroll held by Shannon refers to his election to the Royal Academy in 1911. Ricketts was voted Associate of the Royal Academy in 1922 and became a full Academician in 1928.

Mr Ricketts and Mr Shannon, in the enjoyment of popular success, by Max Beerbohm, 1909. Pen and ink and watercolour. The stern critic is John Bull. Ricketts' sculpture *Orpheus and Eurydice* (plate 76) is caricatured in Max's gloriously malicious manner.

Gordon Bottomley's enquiry about his influence on the *Ballets Russes,* he replied,
'No my dear chap, the Russian designers owe me nothing. My book illustration work has been swamped for ever by the success of Beardsley – whom they know. My stage work, which anticipated much of theirs – the all-red Attila scene, the all-blue Salomé . . . and countless details too

long to describe, such as huge patterns and fantastic head dresses, are unknown to them; they are known here and remembered only by the theatrical profession. Any chance likeness you may detect lies in a common indebtedness to Moreau, or should I say to things initiated and discovered by Moreau; remains a certain local and semi-oriental element which is spontaneous and which with me is replaced by many complex currents of experience. Viewing my theatre work in relation to theirs, I should say that theirs is adventurous and lyric, and mine more intimate and tragic.'

Late years

Some indication of Ricketts' standing in the art world has already been given; this derived not only from the evidence of his expertise as a critic, displayed in his books and articles, but also from his immense reputation as a collector. The ruling passion of Ricketts' life was that rare form of connoisseurship in which the collector's mania is balanced by the scholar's intelligent study of the assembled treasures.

The first great purchase made by Ricketts and Shannon was of a group of Hokusai drawings in 1898. For this they paid the then-great sum of £60. Over a period of thirty years they regularly gave all they had, and frequently more than they could afford, for objects which they wished to own. The size and range of the collection amazed those lucky enough to see it in the small museum it formed first at Lansdowne House and later at Townshend House near Regent's Park. The individual importance of various items made the ultimate fate of the collection a matter of national interest. The National Gallery and the Victoria and Albert Museum had already benefited from time to time from the two artists' generosity, and by the terms of their joint will all the remaining 'treasure' went to public collections, in particular to the Fitzwilliam Museum, Cambridge, where it was their wish that as much of the collection as possible should be shown together.

Sturge Moore records Ricketts' estimate that their income was never more than £1000 a year and usually much less; yet on Ricketts' death in 1931 the collection was valued at £36,203. The explanation lies partly in the fact that they bought wisely in areas which were undervalued; but Ricketts also had a knack for finding unconsidered trifles which it transpired were in fact works of great importance. In this way he had discovered and bought from a

stall for thirty-five shillings the roundel attributed to Masaccio from the *Naples Triptych,* which he gave to the National Gallery.

That Ricketts' concern was not entirely for his own objects is shown in a wonderfully humorous letter to Cecil Smith, then director of the Victoria and Albert Museum, in which he urges that the Museum be closed in view of the impending suffragette riots: 'Please imagine some wild beast of a woman armed with a hammer in the Luca della Robbia room.' If closing was impossible, the only alternative, he suggests, would be to channel the potential danger to where it mattered less. He proposes a sign pointing out the Sèvres display and saying 'This way to the crockery'.

Carrying out a considerable number of duties on various committees and other functions in the art world, Ricketts maintained a genial irony which steered him through much of the bitter controversy of the period. Though he never came to terms with 'modern movements', he won the respect of many through his integrity and enthusiasm as an old-fashioned aesthete: 'With me Art is a function like eating. I choose the dishes I like best; it never occurs to me to taste dishes I dislike, that I may say funny things about them.'

In 1929 Shannon fell while hanging a picture and never fully recovered health or sense. He remained a helpless invalid and for long periods did not recognize Ricketts. The effective loss of his life-long companion was to affect Ricketts badly, but in these last years he found the energy to return to his old love, the production of books. He had continued throughout the years to design the works of his friends, 'Michael Field' and Gordon Bottomley; now, in these final volumes, he is himself revealed as an imaginative writer of some stature. In *Beyond the Threshold* (1929) and *Unrecorded Histories* (1933) Ricketts emerges a lucid stylist in command of a vivid imagery.

In the illustrations for *Beyond the Threshold* and in a second set of designs for *The Sphinx* (unpublished), there is a return to the fantastic and decorative elements of his early work. In the bindings for *Recollections of Oscar Wilde,* and for other individual books to be hand-bound by Sybil Pye, and in the modern silhouette illustrations of *Unrecorded Histories,* there are signs of a whole new idiom of book decoration. Drawing on the refinement of his early exquisite designs, they look unmistakably towards a future development.

'Art has been, Art is. So the present touches wings with the past.'

I *The Death of Montezuma, c.1905.*
Oil on canvas, sight size 75 × 61 cm (30 × 24½ in.).
This picture, one of Ricketts' more successful oils, was originally
in the collection of his patron, Sir Edmund Davis. The story of
Montezuma held a special significance for the artist and he was to
return to the theme many times.

II Design for stage setting for the epilogue of
*Montezuma, c.*1920.
Watercolour, 30·3 × 43·8 cm (11$\frac{7}{8}$ × 17$\frac{1}{16}$ in.).

Ricketts encouraged his young friend Cecil Lewis
to write a dramatic version of Montezuma's last
days, and, though never produced, it remained
one of his favourite theatrical projects. Ricketts
conceived settings of brilliant colours boldly
juxtaposed, exactly expressing the hieratic quality
of the story.

III Design for costume for *Montezuma, c.*1920.
Watercolour, 42·6 × 23·6 cm (16$\frac{3}{4}$ × 9$\frac{1}{4}$ in.).

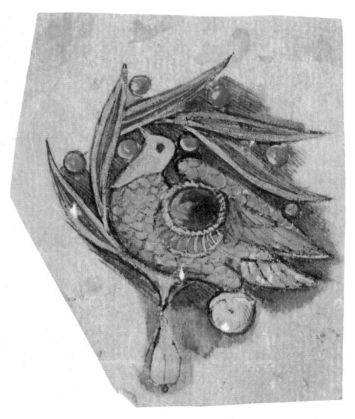

Design and execution

Ricketts, though a prolific designer, always maintained exacting standards and disliked the interpretation of his drawings by others. Thus he engraved most of his own book illustrations and decorations, painted stage backcloths himself and even made stage properties and sewed costumes.

IV, V, 1 Original drawings and wood engraving for illustrations to *The Marriage of Cupide and Psyche*, Vale Press, London 1897.

IV *Love's Pact with Jove.*

Pen and brown ink drawing, touched with white, diameter 7·4 cm (2⅞ in.).

V, 1 *The Descent into Hell.*

IN COLOUR: original pen and brown ink drawing, touched with white. IN BLACK AND WHITE: proof of the wood engraving based on the ink drawing. Diameters 8·3 cm (3¼ in.).

VI, 2 *The Blue Bird,* pendant jewel, *c.*1904.

IN COLOUR: watercolour design from the album *Designs for Jewellery* in the British Museum. IN BLACK AND WHITE: finished jewel in gold and enamel, set with semi-precious stones; made by Ricketts' usual goldsmith Giuliano and intended as a gift for Laurence Binyon's wife. Ricketts was disappointed with the execution and recorded in his diary for 21 May 1904: 'The jewel of bird for Mrs Binyon arrived, it was so hideous and clumsy that I was dumbfounded and depressed . . . gave it to the model, Esther Deacon.'

30

Early work

Many of Ricketts' earliest designs appeared in the illustrated magazines of the 1890s, such as *The Magazine of Art* and *Black and White,* which did much to encourage the work of younger artists.

3 *The Ballad of a shield,* from *The Magazine of Art,* 1892. Overall size 22·9 × 17·3 cm (9 × 6¾ in.). This drawing, clearly based on Burne-Jones' well-known *Holy Grail* tapestries, illustrates a poem by Cosmo Monkhouse.

4 *Vauxhall, 17——,* from *Black and White,* 28 Feb. 1891.

28·8 × 20 cm (11⅜ × 7⅞ in.). An eighteenth-century scene, rare in Ricketts' work, set in the famous pleasure gardens. It recalls the illustrations of Austin Dobson's poems by Hugh Thompson.

5 *Florence,* from *The Magazine of Art,* 1895.
4·3 × 12·8 cm (1¹¹⁄₁₆ × 5 in.). A decorative headpiece in the Aesthetic taste.

6 *A Nympholept,* from *Black and White,* 23 May 1891.

12·5 × 20·5 cm ($4\frac{7}{8}$ × 8 in.). Illustrating a long poem by Augustus Swinburne, *Sleep lies not heavier on eyes that have watched all night Than hangs the heat of noon on the hills and the trees.*

7 *Ariel's song to Ferdinand,* from *The Magazine of Art,* 1895.

23·4 × 15·9 cm ($9\frac{3}{16}$ × $6\frac{1}{4}$ in.). One of a series of designs based on Shakespeare's songs.

Ariel's Song to Ferdinand.

FULL fathom five thy father lies;
  Of his bones are coral made;
Those are pearls that were his eyes:
  Nothing of him that doth fade,
But doth suffer a sea-change
Into something rich and strange.
Sea-nymphs hourly ring his knell:
Hark! now I hear them—ding-dong, bell.

SHAKESPEARE: "THE TEMPEST," *Act I., Scene 2.*

8 *Shelley,* from *The Magazine of Art,* 1892.
Overall size 22·8 × 16·7 cm (9 × $6\frac{1}{2}$ in.). This *tour de force* in the *Symboliste* manner, representing the spirit of Shelley's poetry, illustrates Theodore Watts-Dunton's poem for the Shelley centenary.

THE DIAL
AN OCCASION-
AL PVBLICA-
TION EDITED BY
C. S. RICKETTS &
CH. SHANNON

ICARVS

L. Hacon and Co
Ricketts ~ 52
Warwick Street
Regent Street

 THE accusation was brought against our first Dial of mere art eclecticism ; one thing, keenly attractive to us, might explain this reprehensible selectiveness, a little thing we think common to all good art. Inseparable from the garment of individuality, the word *Document* perfectly explains this.

The Dial

The Dial was the first project over which Ricketts had, with Shannon, complete artistic control. It ran to five numbers, appearing irregularly between 1889 and 1897, and reached a considerable degree of typographic sophistication. In its pages one finds the first really original designs by Ricketts, Shannon and their circle.

9 Cover design for *The Dial,* no. 4, 1896.
Page size 36 × 29·5 cm (14$\frac{1}{4}$ × 11$\frac{5}{8}$ in.). For this fourth number Ricketts redrew the lettering and added the monogram of the Vale Press.

10 *The Unwritten Book,* from *The Dial,* no. 2, 1892.
10·3 × 16 cm (4 × 6$\frac{3}{8}$ in.). The decorative headpiece for Ricketts' manifesto quoted on pp. 13–14.

11 Design for the back cover of *The Dial,* no. 2, 1892. 11·4 × 11·8 cm (4$\frac{1}{2}$ × 4$\frac{5}{8}$ in.).

12 *King James' Lament*, from *The Dial*, no. 5, 1897.
Wood engraving by T. Sturge Moore after a design by Ricketts. Diameter 13 cm (5$\frac{1}{16}$ in.). Intended for the Vale Press edition of *The Kingis Quair*, but not used.

ᔅᴏ Printed at the Ballantyne Press London and Edinburgh.

ᔅᴏ Sold by Charles H Shannon at the Vale in Chelsea.   mdcccxciii.

13 *Sua cum Venustate Renata*, colophon for *The Dial*, no. 3, 1893.
9.8 × 12.5 cm (3$\frac{7}{8}$ × 4$\frac{7}{8}$ in.). The design was first used in *Daphnis and Chloe*, Elkin Mathews and John Lane, London 1893.

14 *Oedipus and the Sphinx*, 1891.
Pen and ink, 23.2 × 20.7 cm (9$\frac{1}{8}$ × 8$\frac{1}{8}$ in.). Commissioned by Lord Leighton for £5 and later bought back by Ricketts, who considered it his finest early drawing.

Commercial book designs

Ricketts' contribution to the world of commercial book production was startlingly original. He popularized the use of unusual formats and inventive typography and brought an eccentric refinement to the design of cloth bindings. As a 'builder of books' his example was influential and his work much imitated.

Poems Dramatic and Lyrical, by Lord de Tabley; Elkin Mathews and John Lane, London 1893 (New York, Macmillan and Co.). Six hundred copies were printed.

15 *Nimrod*
9·7 × 8·7 cm ($3\frac{13}{16}$ × $3\frac{3}{8}$ in.).
Monarch of nations, thou hast conquered much
And always: there is nothing for thy spear.

16 *The Knight in the Wood*
8·6 × 8·6 cm ($3\frac{3}{8}$ × $3\frac{3}{8}$ in.).
... The poor beast with head low-bowed
Snuffing the treacherous ground. The rider leant
Forward to the marish with his lance
You saw the place was deadly; that doomed pair,
The wretched rider and the hide-bound steed,
Feared to advance, feared to return – That's all!

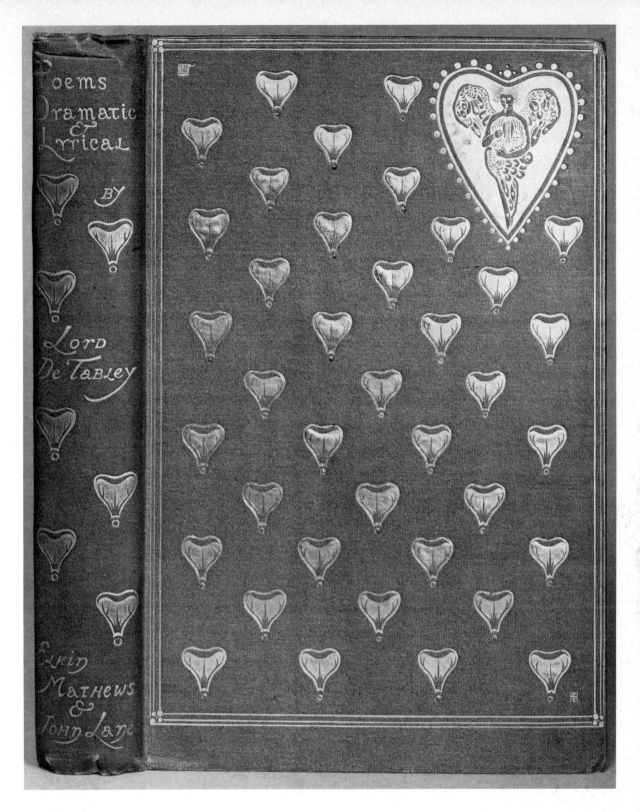

❮ 17 *The Two Old Kings*

9·3 × 8·6 cm (3⅝ × 3⅜ in.).

Brother and King we hold our last carouse
One loving cup we drain and then farewell.

❮ 18 *The Defeat of Glory,*

the original drawing in sepia ink, 9·6 × 8·9 cm (3¾ × 3½ in.).

Yon gaunt image of sepulchral death.

19 Cover,

green cloth blocked in gold, 19·8 × 13 cm (7¹³⁄₁₆ × 5⅛ in.).

Executed by Ricketts' usual binders, Leighton, Son & Hodge.

20 Page ornament from *A House of Pomegranates*, by Oscar Wilde; Osgood and McIlvaine, London 1891. Diameter 2·5 cm (1 in.).

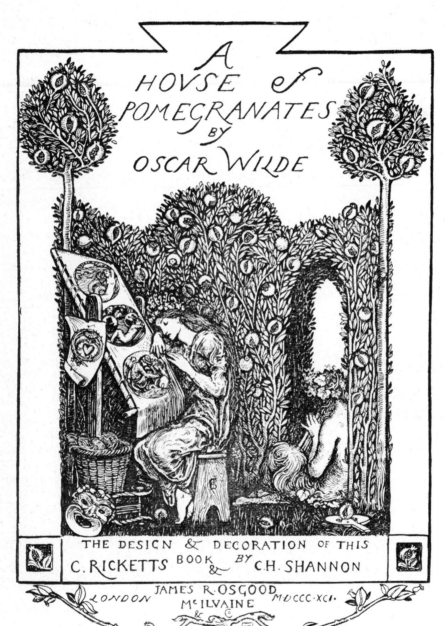

21 Title-page of *A House of Pomegranates*, 1891. Overall size 15 × 10·3 cm (6⅞ × 4 in.).

The Decay of Lying
Pen Pencil & Poison
The Critic as Artist
The Truth of Masks

22 Cover for *A House of Pomegranates*.
Cream cloth blocked in gold
and orange, the spine of green
cloth lettered in gold, 21·9 ×
17·3 cm (8⅝ × 6⅞ in.).

23 Lettering from the cover of *Intentions*,
by Oscar Wilde;
Osgood and McIlvaine, London
1891. 3·5 × 9 cm (1⅛ × 3½ in.).
The titles of the four essays
in the book were blocked in gold
on the green cloth of the cover.

THE FISHER-
-MAN AND
HIS SOVL

TO H.S.H.
ALICE, PRINCESS
OF MONACO.

EVERY evening the young Fisherman went out upon the sea, and threw his nets into the water.

When the wind blew from the land he caught nothing, or but little at best, for it was a bitter and black-winged wind, and rough waves rose up to meet it. But when the wind blew to the shore, the fish came in

63

24 *The Fisherman and his Soul,* opening page of one of the tales in *A House of Pomegranates,* 1891, with illustration, decorative roundel and layout by Ricketts. Page size 21 × 16·7 cm (8¼ × 6½ in.).

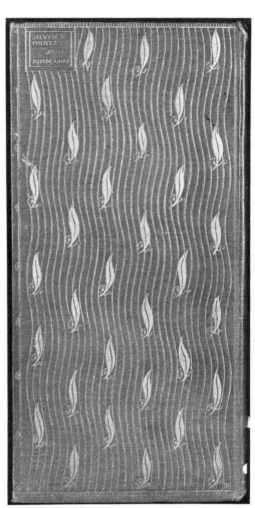

25 Cover for *Silverpoints,* by John Gray; Elkin Mathews and John Lane, London 1893. Blocked in gold on green cloth, 21·7 × 10·8 cm (8 9/16 × 4¼ in.).

26 Cover for *In the Key of Blue,* by J.A. Symonds, Elkin Mathews and John Lane, London 1893. Cream cloth blocked in gold; a few copies were bound in blue cloth, but these are very rare. 22·8 × 17·1 cm (9 × 6¾ in.).

27 *Lovers in a Room,*
c. 1894.
Original pen and ink drawing
for an illustration, 11·2 × 15·6
cm ($4\frac{3}{8}$ × $6\frac{1}{10}$ in.). The
influence of Rossetti is very clear
in drawings of this type.

28 *The Autumn Muse,*
preparatory drawing for wood-
block, pen and ink and white
body colour on tracing paper,
14·1 × 13·4 cm ($5\frac{1}{2}$ × $5\frac{1}{4}$ in.).
Reproduced in *The Pageant,*
1897.

43

WITH DECORATIONS BY CHARLES RICKETTS
LONDON MDCCCXCIV
ELKIN MATHEWS AND JOHN LANE ⸱AT THE SIGN OF THE BODLEY HEAD.

29 *Melancholia*, frontispiece
to *The Sphinx*, 1894.
16 × 12·4 cm ($6\frac{5}{16}$ × $4\frac{7}{8}$ in.).
Perhaps the most perfect of
Ricketts' designs, the page is
printed in three colours – the
image in reddish brown and the
lettering in sage green and black.

The Sphinx

The Sphinx, by Oscar Wilde; Elkin Mathews
and John Lane, London 1894. Page size 21·7 ×
17·1 cm ($8\frac{9}{16}$ × $6\frac{3}{4}$ in.). Ricketts considered his
edition of Wilde's poem the best of his book
designs. It is, indeed, the most harmonious of all
his productions and precisely mirrors the exquisite
and perverse text. Only 250 copies were printed
(50 for America); the greater portion were
destroyed in the Ballantyne Press fire in 1899.

30 Initial letter 'I' from *The Sphinx*, 1894.
4·3 × 4·7 cm ($1\frac{3}{4}$ × $1\frac{7}{8}$ in.).

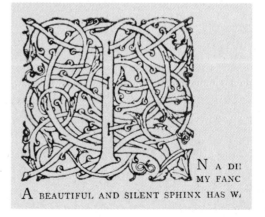

31 *Moon horned Io* from *The Sphinx,* 1894.

7·7 × 12·7 cm (3 × 5 in.).
. . . and did you hear the moon-horned Io weep?

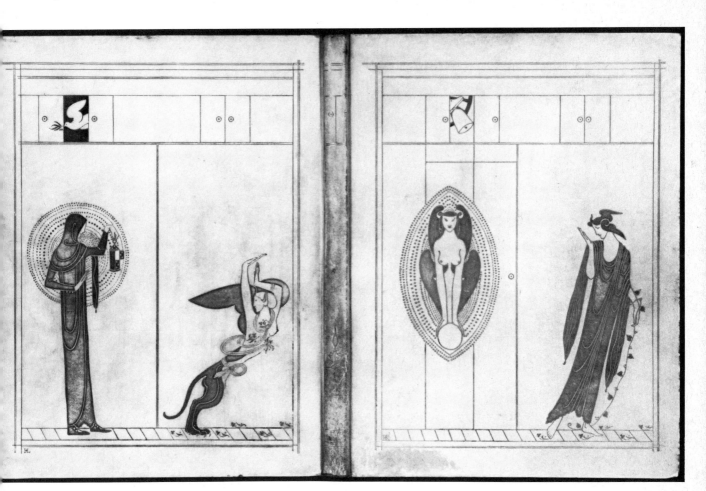

32 Cover of *The Sphinx,* 1894.
Vellum blocked in gold, 22·2 × 17·4 cm (8¾ × 6⅞ in.).
One of 200 copies of the ordinary edition. There were 50 extra copies on large paper, for which extra wavy lines were added to the cover design. This augmented arrangement is less successful than the standard version. The binding was executed as usual by Leighton, Son & Hodge.

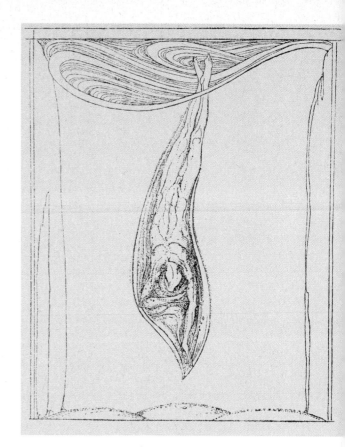

33 *The Fig-tree splits the Pillars of the Peristyle,*
15·4 × 12·2 cm (6 × 4$\frac{13}{16}$ in.).

34 *The Diver of the Colchian Caves,*
15·4 × 11·9 cm (6 × 4$\frac{11}{16}$ in.).

35 *On the Reedy Banks,*
16·5 × 12·5 cm (6$\frac{5}{16}$ × 4$\frac{15}{16}$ in.).

36 *The Labyrinth in which the Twy-formed Bull was
stalled,*
original drawing for illustration to *The Sphinx,* 1894. Pen
and grey ink on pink prepared paper, 19·4 × 16·8 cm
(7$\frac{5}{8}$ × 6$\frac{5}{8}$ in.).

37 *By the Hundred-Cubit Gate Dog-faced Anubis sits in State,* 16·3 × 12·5 cm (6⅜ × 5 in.).

WHOSE PALLID BURDEN, SICK WITH PAIN, WATCHES THE WORLD WITH WEARIED EYES
AND WEEPS FOR EVERY SOUL THAT DIES, AND WEEPS FOR EVERY SOUL IN VAIN.

39 *Pallid Burden, sick with Pain,*
15·3 × 12·4 cm (6 × 4⅞ in.).

38 *The Tyrian,*
16·1 × 12·7 cm (6¼ × 4⅞ in.).

40 *Crouching by the Marge,*
original drawing for illustration to *The Sphinx,* 1894. Pen
and grey ink on pink prepared paper, 20·3 × 16·5 cm (8
× 6½ in.).

THE LOVE OF VENUS FOR ANCHISES

In 1892–94 Ricketts and Shannon collaborated on two illustrated books for which they drew and cut on wood all the illustrations, initial letters and page ornaments. Well printed on good paper, splendidly decorated and issued in distinctive bindings, they mark the final stage to which Ricketts could take the art of designing books for commercial publishing.

Daphnis and Chloe, by Longus, translated by George, Thornley, Gent.; Elkin Mathews and John Lane, London 1893. Two hundred and ten copies were printed. Page size 28·2 × 21 cm ($11\frac{1}{8}$ × $8\frac{1}{4}$ in.).

41 *The Love of Venus for Anchises,*
10·7 × 12·1 cm ($4\frac{3}{16}$ × $4\frac{3}{4}$ in.).

42 Original engraved wood-block for plate 41.
Size of engraved area 10·7 × 12·1 cm ($4\frac{3}{16}$ × $4\frac{3}{4}$ in.). One of the group of Ricketts' and Shannon's blocks preserved in the British Museum Print Room.

THE PASTORAL AMOURS OF DAPHNIS AND CHLOE
THE SECOND BOOK

THE VINTAGE AT MITYLENE

T HE Autumn now being grown to its height, and the Vintage at hand ; every man began to stirre, and be busie in the fields ; some to re-pair the Wine-presses ; some to scowr the tuns, and hogs-heads : others were making baskets, skeps, and panniers ; and others providing little hooks to catch and cut the bunches of the grapes. Here one was looking busily about to find a stone that would serve him to bruise the stones of grapes ; there another, furnishing himself with a stang, of very dry and smooth wood, to carry away the must in the night, with light before him. Wherefore Daphnis and Chloe for this time laid aside the care of the flocks, and put their helping hands to the work. Daphnis in his basket carried grapes, cast them into the presse, and trod them there ; and then anon, out of the Lake, tunn'd the Wine into the Butts. Chloe drest meat for the Vintagers, and served them with drink, the old wine dasht with Fountain-water ; and when she had done, gathered grapes of the lower vines. For all the Vines about Lesbos incline themselves, and protend their palmits towards the ground, and creep like the Ivie ; so that indeed a very infant, if that his hands be loose from his swathes, may easily reach and pull a bunch. Now, as they were wont in the Feast of *Bacchus*, and the solemnization of the *Genethliacs* of wine

1

DAPHNIS FINDS
THE DOLPHIN

and walking there upon the gravell near the line of the ex-cursion and breaking of the waves, he lookt for his three thou-sand Drachma's. But soon he found he should not be put to much labour. For the stench of the Dolphin had reacht him, as he lay cast up, and was rotting upon the slabby sand.

63

43 *The Vintage at Mitylene,*
page size 28·2 × 21 cm ($11\frac{1}{8}$ × $8\frac{1}{4}$ in.).

44 *Daphnis finds the Dolphin,*
page size 28·2 × 21 cm ($11\frac{1}{8}$ × $8\frac{1}{4}$ in.).

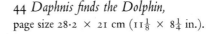

Overleaf
46 *The Rustic Wedding-Feast of Daphnis and Chloe,*
double-page opening from *Daphnis and Chloe*, 1893. Overall size 28·2 × 42 cm ($11\frac{1}{8}$ × $16\frac{1}{2}$ in.). Ricketts included portraits of himself and his friends as guests at the wedding. Seated at the table on the right are (right to left): Ricketts, Shannon, Thomas Sturge Moore, Lucien Pissarro (with a full beard) and Reginald Savage, a talented illustrator in the Vale circle.

45 *How the still singing limbs of the nymph Echo mimicked Pan's voice upon the heights and made the wayward god leap from peak to peak and search about the dells,*
6·9 × 12·2 cm ($2\frac{11}{16}$ × $4\frac{3}{4}$ in.).

habit and, placing him near his own Father, they heard him
speak to this purpose :

I

 MARRIED A WIFE, MY DEAR SONS,
when I was yet very young, and, after a while,
as I conjectured I should, it was my happi-
nesse to be a Father. For first I had a son
born, the second a daughter, and then Astylus
the third. I thought there was enow of the

breed

47 *Daphnis is saved by the fortunate piping of Chloe,*
page size 28·2 × 21 cm (11⅛ × 8¼ in.).

48 *Daphnis plucks from the topmost bough . . . the reddening topmost apple,*
page size 28·2 × 21 cm (11⅛ × 8¼ in.).

49 *The Shepherd Dryas findeth a girl-child in a cave sacred to certain nymphs,*
10·8 × 12·4 cm (4¼ × 4¾ in.).

Hero and Leander, by Christopher Marlowe and George Chapman; Ballantyne Press, Elkin Mathews and John Lane, London 1894. Two hundred and twenty copies were printed. Page size 20 × 13 cm (7¾ × 5⅒ in.).

51 Binding for *Hero and Leander,* 1894.
Vellum blocked in gold, 20·5 × 13 cm (8 1/16 × 5⅒ in.), executed by Leighton, Son & Hodge. The spine bears the Vale Press monogram although the book was actually published by Mathews and Lane.

INTER FOLIA RENATA ROSA

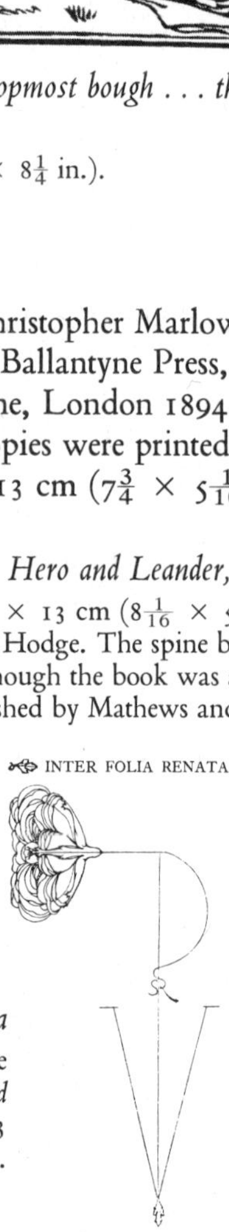

50 *Inter Folia Renata Rosa*
(The Rose reborn between the leaves), colophon from *Hero and Leander,* 1894, page size 20 × 13 cm (7¾ × 5⅒ in.).

HERO AND LEANDER ✤ BY CHRISTOPHER MARLOWE AND GEORGE CHAPMAN

Hero's description and her love's;
The fane of Venus where he moves
His worthy love-suit, and attains;
Whose bliss the wrath of Fates restrains
For Cupid's grace to Mercury:
Which tale the author doth imply.

Illustrations to *Hero and Leander*, 1894.

‹ 52 Frontispiece to *Hero and Leander*, 1894.
Overall size 18 × 11·1 cm (7⅛ × 4¾ in.), illustration 8·3 cm square (3¼ in.).

Then shouldst thou be his prisoner, who is thine.
Be not unkind and fair ; misshapen stuff
Are of behaviour boisterous and rough.
Oh, shun me not, but hear me ere you go !
God knows, I cannot force love as you do :
My words shall be as spotless as my youth,
Full of simplicity and naked truth.
This sacrifice, whose sweet perfume descending

13   From

53 Illuminated page from *Hero and Leander*, 1894.
A single sheet from the book decorated with foliage and other ornament in watercolour and body colour and with an illustration, different from the printed image on the page. A private experiment by Ricketts, found after his death by Sturge Moore amongst the papers of the Vale Press. Page size 20 × 12·8 cm (7¾ × 5 in.).

54 *Neptune quells waves to stay rash Destiny*,
c. 8·3 cm square (3¼ in.).

55 *Leander headlong cleaves enamoured deeps*,
c. 8·3 × 8 cm (3¼ × 3⅛ in.).

56 *Of Venus' flight from spiteful Dian's gibes*,
c. 8·3 cm square (3¼ in.).

Neptune quells waves to stay rash Destiny

Leander headlong cleaves enamoured deeps

Of Venus' flight from spiteful Dian's gibes.

The Vale Press

With the designing and cutting of his own type face, the Vale type, completed Ricketts was ready to pursue an independent course in the publishing world. Supported financially by his partner, the lawyer Llewellyn Hacon, he began to print books in 1896. In all, 44 works were issued, together with a 39-volume edition of Shakespeare. The last book which Ricketts produced was a bibliography of the Vale Press in 1904.

57 *Nimphidia and the Muses Elizium,* by Michael Drayton,
Vale Press, London 1896. Page size 23·5 × 14·5 cm (9⅛ × 5⅛ in.). The frontispiece depicts Oberon, King of the Fairies.

I T IS NOW SEVEN YEARS SINCE THE FIRST BOOK WAS PUBLISHED BY HACON & RICKETTS. THREE SEPARATE FOUNTS HAVE BEEN DESIGNED AND ISSUED BY THEM, THE VALE FOUNT, THE AVON FOUNT, AND THE KING'S FOUNT. AS IT IS UNDESIRABLE THAT THESE FOUNTS SHOULD DRIFT INTO OTHER HANDS THAN THEIR DESIGNERS' AND BECOME STALE BY UNTHINKING USE, IT HAS BEEN DECIDED TO DESTROY THE PUNCHES, MATRICES, AND TYPE

58 *A Bibliography of Books Published by Hacon and Ricketts,*

Vale Press, London 1904. Page size 22 × 14·5 cm ($8\frac{1}{4}$ × $5\frac{5}{8}$ in.). The frontispiece shows the sign board painted by Charles Shannon for the Vale Press office in Warwick Street, *c.* 1896. It represents 'the Dial' and below, Pegasus grazing in an enclosed paddock.

59 Original pen and ink drawings for page ornaments, various sizes.

60 *The Shipwreck,* projected illustrations for *The Kingis Quair*

(issued without illustration), Vale Press, London 1903. Each 20·3 × 14·5 cm ($8\frac{3}{8}$ × $5\frac{11}{16}$ in.). Reproduced in *The Dial,* no. 4, 1896, from the original drawings.

61 *The Prodigal Son,* from *The Parables,*

Vale Press, London 1903. 85 × 77 cm ($33\frac{1}{2}$ × $30\frac{3}{8}$ in.). One of a set of ten illustrations. The design is perhaps influenced by Dürer's vision of the subject.

60

Illustrations from *De Cupidinis et Psyches amoribus*, Vale Press, 1901. Ricketts' second version of the story printed in Latin.

62 *Psyche in the House*, 9·4 × 8·6 cm ($3\frac{11}{16}$ × $3\frac{3}{8}$ in.).

63 *The Flight of Cupid*, 10 × 8·6 cm ($3\frac{7}{8}$ × $3\frac{3}{8}$ in.).

64 *Danaë at her twilit lattice ponders,* from
Danaë, A Poem, by T. Sturge Moore,
Vale Press, London 1903. 11 × 7·5 cm (4$\frac{5}{16}$
× 2$\frac{11}{16}$ in.). The lettering above the illustration,
printed in red, is set in Ricketts' last designed
type, the hybrid King's Fount.

65 Illustration for a projected Vale Press
edition of Plato's *Symposion,* n.d.
From a unique proof, 12·2 × 8·2 cm (4$\frac{3}{4}$ × 3$\frac{3}{16}$
in.). The title in Greek lettering is hand drawn
and engraved with the image.

66 Page of text with 'Renaissance'
decoration from *The World at Auction,* by
'Michael Field',
Vale Press, London 1893. Page size 24 × 14·5
cm (9$\frac{5}{16}$ × 5$\frac{11}{16}$ in.).

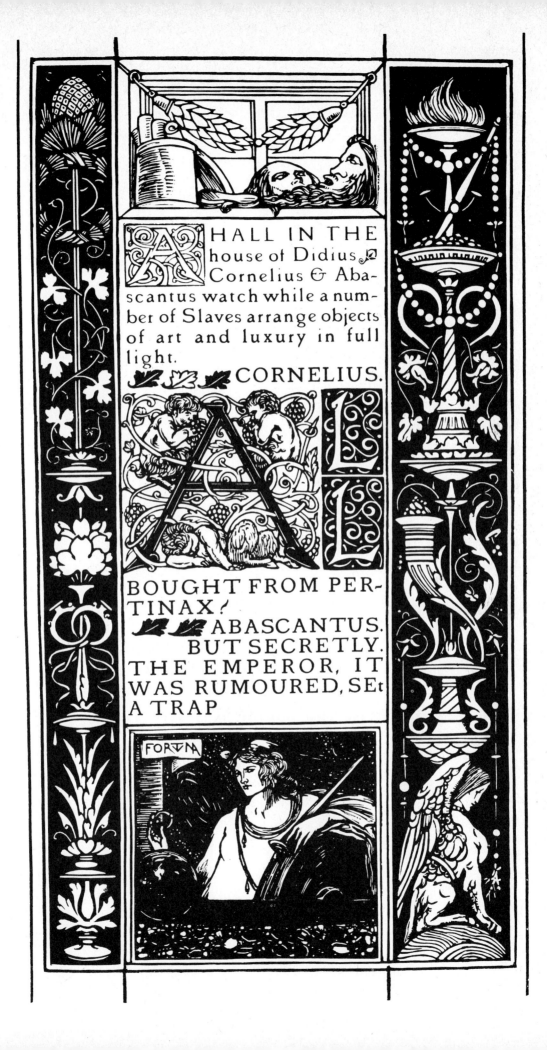

A HALL IN THE house of Didius. Cornelius & Abascantus watch while a number of Slaves arrange objects of art and luxury in full light.

CORNELIUS.

ALL BOUGHT FROM PERTINAX?

ABASCANTUS. BUT SECRETLY. THE EMPEROR, IT WAS RUMOURED, SEt A TRAP

FORVM

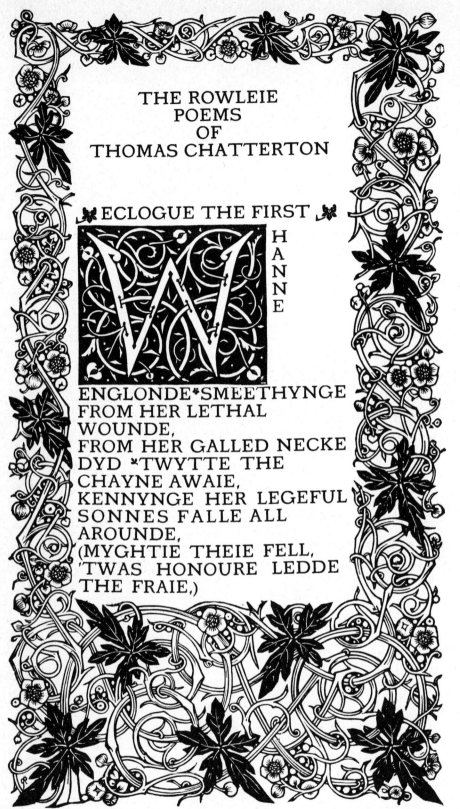

THE ROWLEIE
POEMS
OF
THOMAS CHATTERTON

ECLOGUE THE FIRST

WHANNE ENGLONDE∗SMEETHYNGE
FROM HER LETHAL
WOUNDE,
FROM HER GALLED NECKE
DYD ∗TWYTTE THE
CHAYNE AWAIE,
KENNYNGE HER LEGEFUL
SONNES FALLE ALL
AROUNDE,
(MYGHTIE THEIE FELL,
'TWAS HONOURE LEDDE
THE FRAIE,)

67 *The Rowleie (Rowley) Poems,* by Thomas Chatterton,
Vale Press, London 1898. Opening page of text with decorative border, *Wild Briony,* and initial letter, 23 × 14·3 cm (9⅛ × 5⅝ in.).

68 Binding for *The Rowley Poems,* 1898,
in two patterned papers, *Grapes* and *Bird and Bough,* designed by Ricketts. 23·7 × 14·7 cm (9⅜ × 5¾ in.).

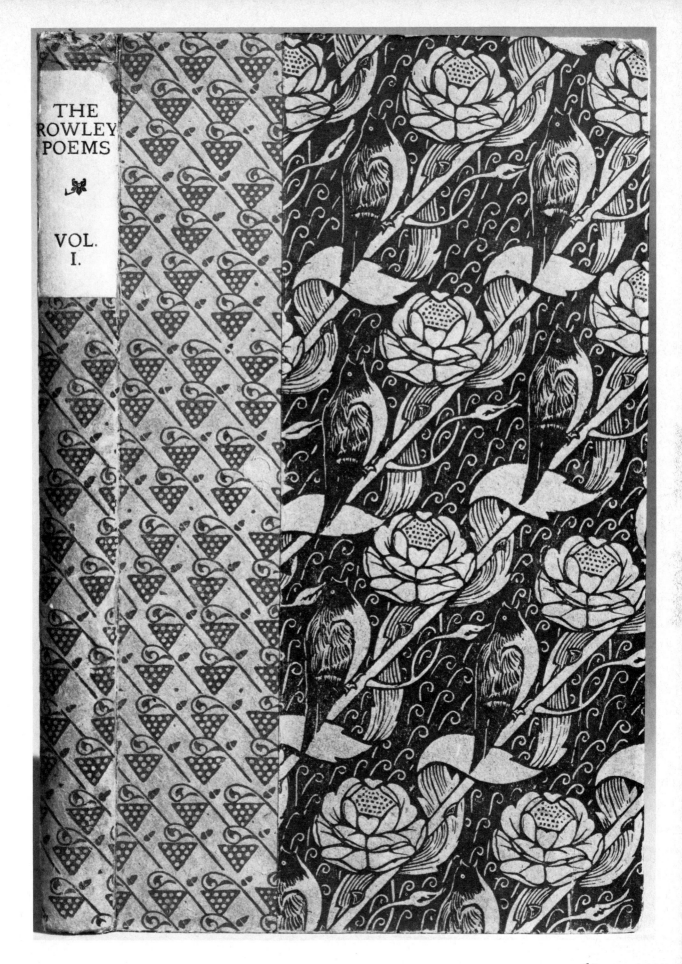

THE
ROWLEY
POEMS

VOL.
I.

Painting

With the move to Lansdowne House in 1903 Ricketts again turned to oil painting, finding it no easier than before. His increasing knowledge of the works and techniques of the Italian and Spanish masters apparently only complicated his problems with form and colour.

69 *The Resurrection of the Dead, c.* 1903. Oil on canvas, 76·2 × 63·6 cm (30 × 25 in.). Exhibited at the New Gallery, 1908.

70 *A Fancy Dress Party, c.* 1903. Oil on canvas, 16·5 × 22·5 cm ($6\frac{1}{2}$ × $8\frac{7}{8}$ in.). An unusual modern subject drawn from life, the scene is an entertainment given by Sir Edmund Davis. Said to be shown (left to right) are: Mrs Edmund Davis, Sir Edmund, Mrs Charles Conder, Max Beerbohm, Miss Halford, Charles Conder and Ricketts.

71 *The Betrayal of Christ,* 1904.
Oil on canvas, 91·4 × 71·1 cm (36 × 28 in.). One of the
most successful of Ricketts' oil paintings, it was exhibited at
the International Exhibition in Rome, 1911, and at the
Royal Academy in 1933.

72 *Darius rising from the Tomb, c.* 1913.

Lithograph, 61·4 × 43·5 cm (24$\frac{3}{16}$ × 17$\frac{1}{8}$ in.). Ricketts' surviving lithographs clearly reflect the influence of Odilon Redon in both subject and treatment.

73 *The Dynasts,* 1914.   Lithograph, 60·2 × 46·7 cm (23$\frac{11}{16}$ × 18$\frac{3}{8}$ in.). Used as a poster advertising Thomas Hardy's play *The Dynasts,* produced by H. Granville Barker at the Kingsway Theatre with decorations by Ricketts, 25 November 1914.

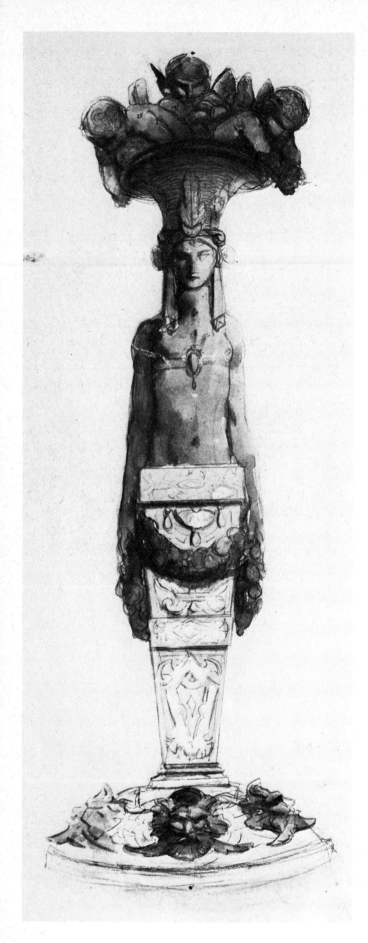

Sculpture and jewellery

Ricketts took up the modelling of small bronzes partly in admiration of Rodin, the leading sculptor of the day, but partly also as a relief from his struggle with oil painting. The pieces of jewellery made to Ricketts' designs in these years often seem like sculpture on a minute scale, a characteristic they share with the vigorous and colourful Renaissance and Baroque gems which he so admired.

74 *Design for a Fountain,* c. 1910.

Pen and wash, 35·3 × 20·1 cm (13$\frac{7}{8}$ × 7$\frac{3}{8}$ in.). The fountain was to be cast in bronze for the dark courtyard of Chilham Castle, Kent. Chilham was the country residence of Sir Edmund Davis who let the old keep to Ricketts and Shannon as a retreat. A fountain of similar form is still at Chilham.

75 *Silence,* bronze, c. 1906. From an old photograph.

76 *Orpheus and Eurydice,* 1905–07.

Plaster, 33·7 × 24·2 × 15·3 cm (13$\frac{1}{4}$ × 9$\frac{1}{2}$ × 6 in.). The original plaster model for the bronze group, of which an example is in the Tate Gallery. This version was given by Ricketts to Cecil Lewis.

77 *Pendant Jewel*, 1900.
Gold and enamel set with semi‚
precious stones and Baroque
pearls. Made to Ricketts' designs
by Giuliano for Mrs Llewellyn
Hacon, the wife of Ricketts'
partner in the Vale Press
enterprise. Ricketts modelled the
gold portrait medallion 'with
knife and lead pencil'.

78 *Design for a Jewel*.
Ink and watercolour, irregular,
actual size. This working
drawing for the *Pegasus* pendant
made for Edith Cooper
('Michael Field') is one of the
collection of Ricketts' *Designs for
Jewellery* preserved in the British
Museum Album.

Theatre designs

Ricketts' involvement with theatre design from a modest beginning before the First World War rapidly came to occupy most of his creative energies. In the last twenty years of his life he produced several hundred large finished watercolour designs for costumes and stage settings.

79 Design for stage setting of *King Lear* (Lear's Palace).

Pencil and wash, 36·7 × 52·1 cm (14 × $20\frac{7}{16}$ in.). Produced by Herbert Trench, Theatre Royal, Haymarket, 8 Sept. 1909.

80 Design for stage setting of Aeschylus' *The Eumenides, c.* 1919.

Pencil and wash 41·8 × 57·2 cm ($16\frac{1}{2}$ × $22\frac{1}{2}$ in.). One of Ricketts' most splendidly hieratic conceptions.

81 Costume design for *Judith*.

Pencil and wash, 38·1 × 30·5 cm (15 × 12 in.). This design for Judith, in the play of the same name by Arnold Bennett produced at the Kingsway Theatre on 30 April 1919, was not passed for public exhibition and a more 'decent' version had to be substituted.

82 Lillah McCarthy as Judith,
showing the first version of the costume before alteration.

83 Costume design for Leontes, *c.* 1925.

Pencil and wash, 36·8 × 73·4 cm ($14\frac{1}{2}$ × $5\frac{1}{4}$ in.). For a projected production of Shakespeare's *The Winter's Tale*.

86 Costume design for ⟩
Buffon, for a projected
production of *Sakuntala*.

86 Costume design for
Buffon, for a projected
production of *Sakuntala*.
Pencil and watercolour, 38·8 ×
28·2 cm (15¼ × 11¹⁄₁₀ in.). This
oriental extravanganza was never
produced.

84 Design for stage setting
for a projected production
of *Parsifal*.

85 Costume design for
Tristan, *c.* 1921.
For a projected production of
Tristan and Isolde. Pencil and
watercolour, 41·5 × 26·1 cm
(16³⁄₈ × 10¼ in.).

The gloomy keep at
Chilham Castle provided
the inspiration for Ricketts'
series of designs for
Wagner's operas,
commissioned in about
1920 for the Bayreuth
Festival by the tenor,
Melchoir, but never used.

87 Costume design for the ceremonial robe of
Katisha in *The Mikado*, by Gilbert and Sullivan.
Watercolour, 48·8 × 70·3 cm (19$\frac{3}{16}$ × 27$\frac{5}{8}$ in.). Ricketts'
most successful production for the D'Oyly Carte
Company. He stencilled the Japanese patterns on the
costumes single-handed. Staged at the Prince's Theatre,
September 1926.

88 Costume design for the Witch Dancer for a
projected production of *Itto*.
Pencil and watercolour, 37·7 × 27·1 cm (14$\frac{7}{8}$ × 10$\frac{5}{8}$ in.).
Ricketts' love of Japanese art led him to share W.B. Yeats'
interest in the Japanese theatre, in particular Noh drama.

90 Costume design for a dancer for *Judith*, by
Arnold Bennett, 1919.
Pencil and watercolour, 39·3 × 31·2 cm (15$\frac{7}{16}$ × 12$\frac{1}{4}$ in.).

⟨89 Costume design for a Shakespearian heroine,
probably Beatrice in *Much Ado About Nothing*, *c.* 1919.
Pencil and watercolour, 35·9 × 27·7 cm (14$\frac{1}{8}$ × 10$\frac{9}{10}$
in.). One of the group of drawings contributed by Ricketts
to the Shakespeare Memorial Theatre Fund. The series was
published in book form as *Shakespeare's Heroines* (London n.d.).

St Joan, by George Bernard Shaw, produced by the author and Lewis Casson at the New Theatre, March 1924. The production was commemorated by an edition of the play illustrated with Ricketts' designs.

91 Design for the tapestry drop-curtain, *Love.* Pen and ink, 39·4 × 59·6 cm (15½ × 23⅜ in.).

92 Costume designs for two court ladies for *St Joan,* 1924. Watercolour, 35·6 × 27·4 cm (14 × 10¾ in.).

93 Group of characters in costume in front of the tapestry drop-curtain, 1924. Production photograph by Beresford.

94 Costume design for the Dumb Wife, from *The Man who married a Dumb Wife,* by Anatole France.

Watercolour, 38·8 × 27·4 cm (15¼ × 10¾ in.). The play was produced in 1915 in New York and later at the Ambassador's Theatre, London, January 1917. Ricketts designed only this dress in the play, for the actress Lillah McCarthy.

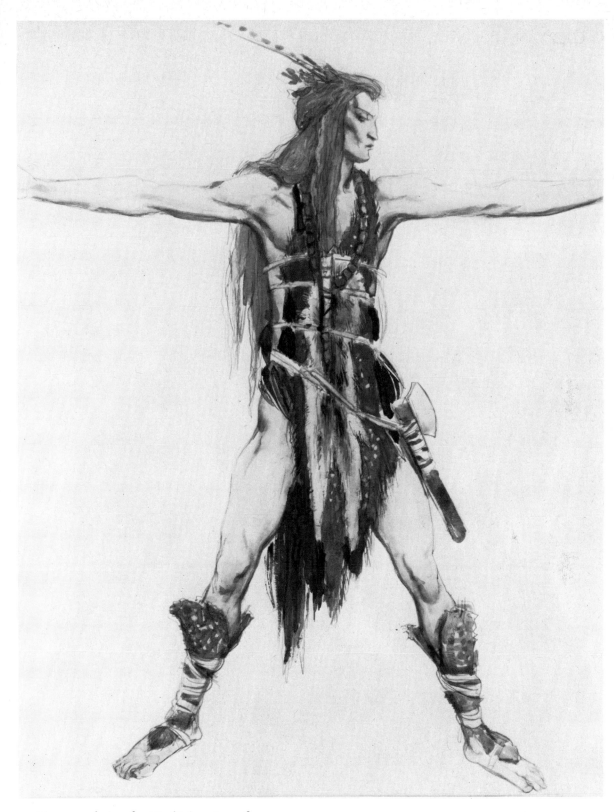

96 Costume design for *Siegfried, c.* 1921, for a
projected production of Wagner's opera.
Watercolour, 41·5 × 26·1 cm ($16\frac{3}{8}$ × $10\frac{1}{4}$ in.).

95 Costume design for the Young Syrian for
Salomé by Oscar Wilde.
Watercolour 26·7 × 21·6 cm ($10\frac{1}{2}$ × $8\frac{1}{2}$ in.). A replica
of the lost original design for the Tokyo production of 1919.

After Oscar Wilde's death Ricketts became increasingly devoted to his memory. He paid tribute to the friendship which was so important to him during the years at the Vale in the delightful *Recollections of Oscar Wilde* (published posthumously in 1932) and in two groups of illustrations for Wilde's writings. These were a second set of designs for *The Sphinx* and a series for *Poems in Prose*. The *Sphinx* designs, whilst related to the 1894 edition, are completely reworked in Ricketts' new manner, and the *Poems in Prose* drawings are in the style which he evolved for his own *Beyond the Threshold* (1929).

97 *The Birth of Pandora*, from *Beyond the Threshold*, 1929.
The original pen and ink drawing, 23 × 16·8 cm (9$\frac{1}{16}$ × 6$\frac{5}{8}$ in.).

98 *Judas Iscariot*, from *Beyond the Threshold*, 1929.
The original pen and ink drawing, 21·1 × 15·1 cm (8$\frac{5}{16}$ × 5$\frac{5}{8}$ in.).

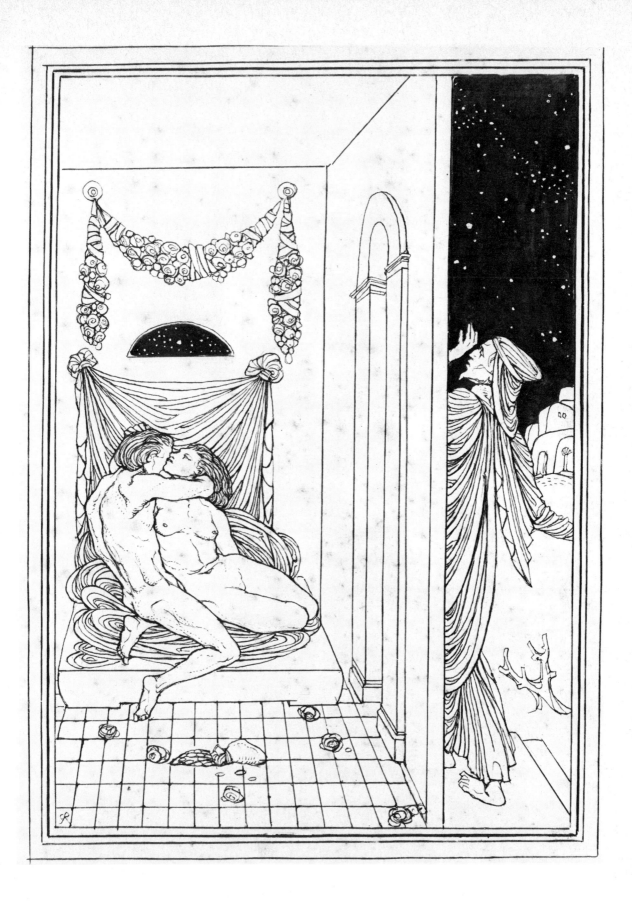

99–104 Original pen and ink drawings, a second
series of illustrations to *The Sphinx,* by Oscar Wilde.

99 . . . *the Painted Swathèd Dead,*
22·7 × 15·1 cm (9 × 6 in.).

100 . . . *River Horses in the Slime,*
20·7 × 15·1 cm ($8\frac{3}{16}$ × 6 in.).

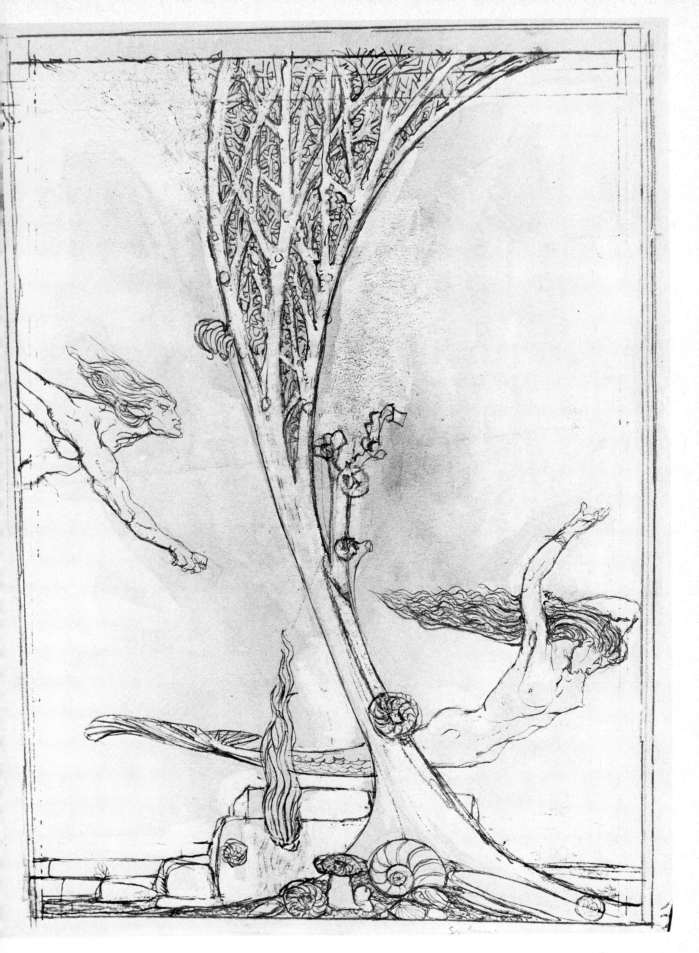

101 . . . *the Painted Kings who Sleep beneath the Wedge-shaped Pyramid,*
20·8 × 10·2 cm ($8\frac{3}{16}$ × 4 in.).

102 . . . *the Labyrinth in which the Twy-formed Bull was Stalled,*
20 × 14·2 cm ($7\frac{7}{8}$ × $5\frac{5}{8}$ in.).

103 . . . *on his Ivory Breast there Shone the*
Wondrous Ocean Emerald, 22 × 15·8 cm (8$\frac{11}{16}$ × 6$\frac{1}{4}$ in.).

104 . . . *you made the Horned God your Own,*
19·6 × 14·2 cm (7¾ × 5⅝ in.).

Final years

In his final years, Ricketts developed an entirely new idiom of book design and illustration. Using elements from his books of thirty years before, it is as modern in style as the work of many of the designers represented in the Paris Exhibition of Decorative Arts, 1925.

105 Bookplate for John Morgan, *c.* 1925.
Original drawing for the bookplate engraved under Ricketts supervision by Bernard Sleigh. This design, which is unusual in both style and sentiment, resembles closely the work of Eric Gill.

106 Cover for *Oscar Wilde, Recollections by . . . Charles Ricketts,*
Nonesuch Press, London 1932. Cream cloth blocked in gold, 25·7 × 16·2 cm (10¼ × 6⅜ in.). The design is a re-working of the *Sphinx* binding of 1894.

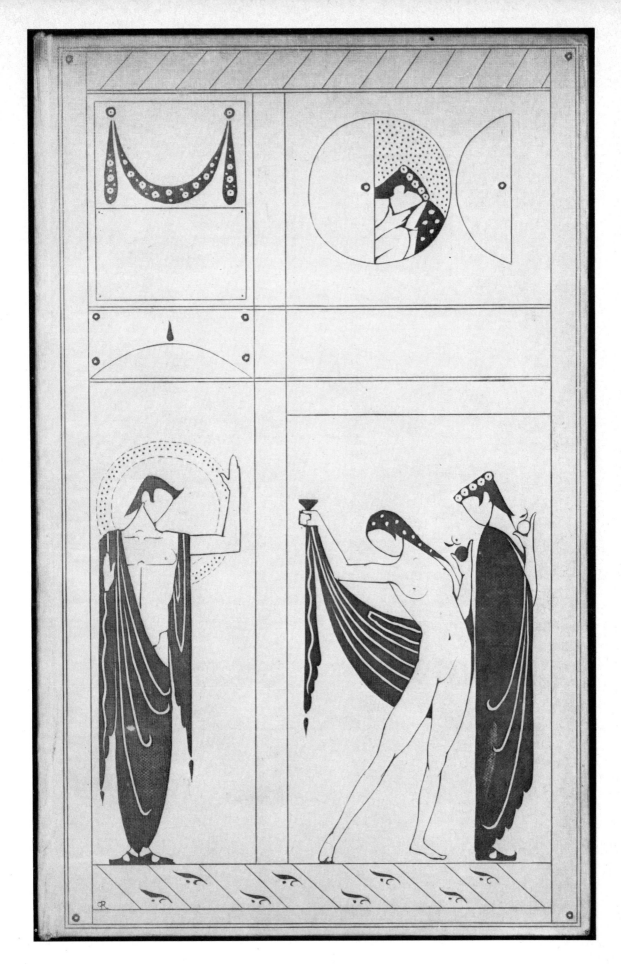

Illustrations in silhouette from *Unrecorded Histories* by Charles Ricketts, published posthumously by Martin Secker, London 1933. These 'modernistic' designs are printed in reddish brown.

107 *The Transit of the Gods,*
15·1 × 10·2 cm (5$\frac{15}{16}$ × 4 in.).

108 *The Pavilion of the Winds,*
15·4 × 10·2 cm (6 × 4 in.).

109 Binding for *Beyond the Threshold,* by Jean ⟩
Paul Raymond,
translated from the French and Illustrated by Charles Ricketts. Privately Printed. Published under Ricketts' pseudonym of Raymond and printed by the Curwen Press, 1929. Maroon morocco leather, blocked in gold, 26·8 × 18 cm (10$\frac{1}{2}$ × 7$\frac{1}{8}$ in.). The elegant geometric design of the cover is similar to those executed in the 1920s by the binder Sybil Pye after drawings by Ricketts.

94

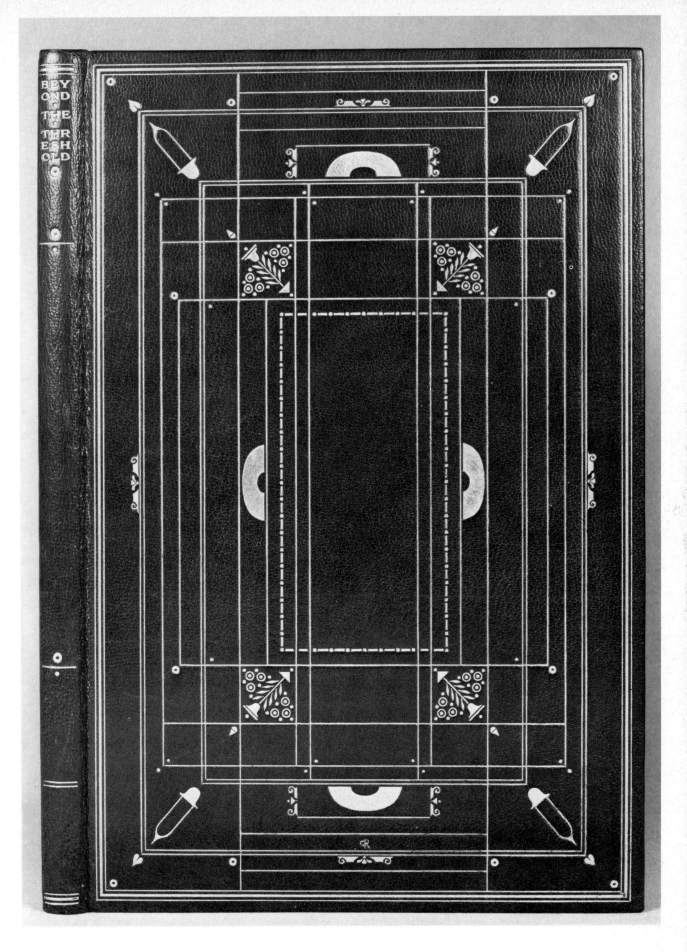

110 Initial letter and *culs-de-lampe* designed and engraved by Ricketts, *c.* 1893–98, various sizes.

MDCCC
XCVI

MDCM
IV

111 Wood engraver's burin, from the colophon of
the *Bibliography* of the Vale Press, 1904.

Select bibliography

MAIN SOURCES

Art Ancien, *Bulletin 25: A Collection of books designed by Charles Ricketts*, Zurich 1972.

BARBER, Giles, 'Rossetti, Ricketts and Some English Publishers' Bindings of the 'Nineties', *The Library*, series 5, XXV (1970).

BEHMER, Marcus, 'Charles Ricketts', *Buchkunst*, vol. 2 (1935).

CALLOWAY, Stephen and DELANEY, Paul, *Charles Ricketts and Charles Shannon*, A Catalogue of the Exhibition at Orleans House, Twickenham, March 1979.

DELANEY, Paul, 'Father of the Well-made book', *Country Life*, 23 Jan. 1975.
'Charles Ricketts', *Antiquarian Book Monthly Review*, vol. V, no. 7 (1978).
'Book design; a nineteenth century Revival', *Connoisseur*, August 1978.

FLETCHER, Ifan, 'Charles Ricketts and the Theatre', *Theatre Notebook*, 1966.

FRENCH, Cecil, 'The wood engravings of Charles Ricketts', *Print Collector's Quarterly*, 14 (1927).

GALLATIN, A. E., *An Exhibition of Books designed by Charles Ricketts from the collection of A. E. Gallatin*, The Houghton Library, Harvard University, 1946.

HIND, Lewis, 'Charles Ricketts, a commentary on his activities, *Studio Magazine*, XLVIII, no. 202 (1910).

LOWINSKY, Thomas, 'Charles Ricketts', *Dictionary of National Biography 1931–1940*, Oxford 1949.

MOORE, T. Sturge, *Charles Ricketts, Sixty-five designs*, London 1933.

RICKETTS, Charles, Diaries and Journals (unpub.), in Dept of Manuscripts, British Library.
'A note on original wood engraving', *The Pageant* (1897).
A Defence of the Revival of Printing, Vale Press, London 1899.
A Bibliography of Books Published by Hacon and Ricketts, Vale Press, London 1904.
Oscar Wilde, Recollections . . ., Nonesuch Press, London 1932.
Self-Portrait, letters and journals collected and compiled by T. Sturge Moore, edited by Cecil Lewis, London 1939.

(ed. Delaney, P.), *Michael Field* (a memoir), Tragara Press, Edinburgh 1976.
(ed. Delaney, P.), *Pages from a Diary in Greece*, Tragara Press, Edinburgh 1978.

SUTTON, Denys, 'A Neglected Virtuoso: Charles Ricketts and his Achievements', *Apollo*, 83 (1966).

WHITE, Gleeson, 'The Work of Charles Ricketts', *The Pageant* (1896).
'At the sign of the Dial, Mr. Ricketts as a book builder', *Magazine of Art* (1897).

SECONDARY SOURCES

CAVE, Roderick, *The Private Press*, London 1971.

CLARK, Kenneth, *Another Part of the Wood*, London 1974.

CRANE, Walter, *Decorative Illustration*, London 1896.

DELANEY, Paul, *The Lithographs of Charles Shannon*, Taranman Gallery, London 1978.

'FIELD, Michael', *Works and Days*, London 1933.

FRANKLIN, Colin, *The Private Presses*, London 1969.

FURST, Herbert, 'The Modern Woodcut. Part II', *The Print Collector's Quarterly*, 8 (1921).

GERE, Charlotte, *Victorian Jewellery Design*, London 1972.

HART-DAVIES, Rupert, *The Caricatures of Max Beerbohm*, London 1970.

HOLMES, Charles J., *Self and Partners (Mostly Self)*, New York 1936.

HONE, J., *W. B. Yeats*, Harmondsworth 1971 (first published 1942).

HOUGHTON *Library, The Turn of a Century*, Art Nouveau-Jugendstil Books, Dept of Printing & Graphic Arts, The Houghton Library, Harvard University, 1970. (Introduction by Peter A. Wick).

HOUSMAN, Laurence, *The Unexpected Years*, London 1937.

JACKSON, Holbrook, *The Eighteen Nineties*, London 1922.

KENNET, Lady, *Self-portrait of an Artist*, London 1949.

LEWIS, Cecil, *Never Look Back*, London 1974.

LUCIE-SMITH, E., *Symbolist Art*, London 1972.
MASON, Stuart, *Bibliography of Oscar Wilde*, with a note by Robert Ross, 2 vols., London 1914. Reprinted in 1 vol. by Bertram Rota, London 1970.
MUIR, Percy, *Victorian Illustrated Books*, London 1971.
PENNEL, Joseph, *Modern Illustration*, London 1895.
ROSS, Robert, *Friend of Friends*, letters to Robert Ross, Art Critic and Writer, edited by Margery Ross, London 1952.
ROTHENSTEIN, John, *The Artists of the 1890's*, London 1928.
ROTHENSTEIN, William, *Men and Memories*, vol. I, 1872–1900, London 1934.
STEELE, Robert, *The Revival of Printing*, a bibliographical catalogue of works issued by the chief modern English presses, London 1912.
SYMONS, A. J. A., 'An Unacknowledged Movement in Fine Printing. The Typography of the Eighteen-Nineties', *The Fleuron*, VII (1930).
TAYLOR, John Russell, *The Art Nouveau Book in Britain*, London 1966.
THORPE, James, *English Illustration: The Nineties*, London 1935.
UZANNE, Octave, *L'Art dans la décoration extérieure des livres en France et à l'étranger*, Paris 1898.
WEITENKAMPF, Rudolf, *The Illustrated Book*, London 1938.
WHITE, Colin, *Edmund Dulac*, London 1976.
WHITE, Gleeson, 'The Artistic Decoration of Cloth Book-Covers', *The Studio*, IV (1894).

Acknowledgments

I would like to thank Miss Henriette Sturge Moore and Mr Daniel Sturge Moore, Ricketts' executors, for permission to quote and reproduce copyright material.

A number of friends and colleagues have given me their assistance in the preparation of these pages: at the Victoria and Albert Museum, Lionel Lambourne and Michael Snodin; Frances Carey of the British Museum Print Room, John Goldfinch of the British Library, Patricia Astley-Cooper of Orleans House Gallery and Penny Shimmin at the City Art Gallery, Carlisle; Stephen Jones, John Lewis, Simon Reynolds, John Westbrook and Cecil Lewis.

My greatest debt is to Paul Delaney, whose constant interest and comments have helped me at every stage of my work.

The greater portion of the illustrations were specially photographed for this book by John Lee.

Illustrations are reproduced by kind permission of the following owners:

Ashmolean Museum, Oxford, pls. 36, 40, 77, 86, 88–90, 96; Bodleian Library, Oxford, p. 15, pl. 26; British Library, p. 12 *below*; British Museum, pls. VI, 18, 28, 42, 53, 64, 65, 78; Carlisle City Art Gallery (Gordon Bottomley Bequest), *title-page*, pls. 14, 27, 59, 69, 71–74, 85, 97–105; Messrs P. & D. Colnaghi, London, pl. 61; Derby Museum and Art Gallery, pl. 81; Fitzwilliam Museum, Cambridge, *frontispiece*, p. 23 *above* and *below*, pls. 2, 91; National Portrait Gallery, p. 20; Private Collections, pp. 7, 9, 11 *below*, 19 *below*, 22, pls. 3–8, 15–17, 19, 20–24, 66–68, 75, 76, 106–110; Simon Reynolds, pl. I; Victoria and Albert Museum, *half-title*, pp. 11 *above*, 12 *above*, 19 *above*, pls. II–V, 1, 9–13, 25, 29–35, 37–39, 41, 43–52, 54–58, 60, 62, 63, 79, 80, 82–84, 87, 92–95, 111.

Index

99